'This is a treasure trove, a gold mine, a Christmas-every-day cornucopia of rich Australian history, particularly Second World War history. Arguments over the "Brisbane Line" are settled here. Now we have the detailed plans for the "scorched earth" tactic that might follow a Japanese invasion of Australia. We know that Sydney, Melbourne, Brisbane and Canberra were to be defended at all costs: too bad if you lived in Darwin, Perth, Adelaide or Hobart, still worse if you lived in Alice Springs or Townsville. Outside the big four cities, Australians could expect evacuation if all else looked like failing. The detail is mind-boggling: how to sabotage water supplies; how to wreck a car; a safe walking route from Grafton to Glen Innes; how to "trip" a tank with a crowbar. Read . . . and wonder!'

PETER GROSE, AUTHOR OF *AN AWKWARD TRUTH* AND *A VERY RUDE AWAKENING*

AUSTRALIA'S SECRET PLAN FOR TOTAL WAR UNDER
JAPANESE INVASION IN WORLD WAR II

SCORCHED EARTH

EDITED BY
SUE ROSEN

ALLEN&UNWIN
SYDNEY • MELBOURNE • AUCKLAND • LONDON

First published in 2017

Allen & Unwin
83 Alexander Street
Crows Nest NSW 2065
Australia
Phone: (61 2) 8425 0100
Email: info@allenandunwin.com
Web: www.allenandunwin.com

Cataloguing-in-Publication details are available
from the National Library of Australia
www.trove.nla.gov.au

ISBN 978 1 92557 514 9

Set in 11/15 pt Sabon by Midland Typesetters, Australia
Printed and bound in Australia by Griffin Press

10 9 8 7 6 5 4 3 2

The paper in this book is FSC® certified. FSC® promotes environmentally responsible, socially beneficial and economically viable management of the world's forests.

CONTENTS

Commissioner E.H.F. Swain

PREFACE

One of my favourite places is the reading room of State Records New South Wales in western Sydney, where one can make the most unexpected and delightful discoveries. As a historian and heritage consultant, I've spent entire weeks there, poring over old files, photos, maps and surveyor's sketches. In January 2012, I was researching the Murray River Red Gum forests of southern New South Wales for the NSW National Parks and Wildlife Service when I called up Forestry Commission file 3/5944. It turned out to have nothing to do with Red Gum forests, but instead detailed the 'Wartime Activities of the Forestry Commission' by a subcommittee headed by NSW Forestry Commissioner E.H.F. Swain. Glancing through the first few pages, I read phrases such as 'Total War' and 'Battle Stations for All' and 'Defence in Depth'. As I read on, it dawned on me that I had found buried treasure. These somewhat tatty, yellowing papers detailed plans for implementing in New South Wales the 'scorched earth' policy adopted in 1942 by the Curtin government amid fears of an imminent Japanese invasion.

To say I was distracted is an understatement—it was a wonderful find, the kind that sets your heart racing. I could not and did not let it go. As soon as I had time to spare, I revisited the file and began seeking references to 'scorched earth' elsewhere. Although, the Scorched Earth Code (or, as it became known, the 'Denial of Resources to the Enemy' policy) was a federal initiative, very little on the policy can be found in National Archives using 'scorched earth' as a search term.

On closer investigation, I also realised that the Forestry file was incomplete, but I was fortunate to track down missing policy components, in State Records' Premier's Department files at 8/2147, via correspondence between Premier William McKell and Commissioner Swain. While the Scorched Earth Code presented here is complete, other related correspondence may exist in the archives of other departments such as the NSW Department of Main Roads, who were required to implement aspects of the policy.

The original documents are foolscap, typewritten roneoed sheets. They set out the rationale for the Scorched Earth Code and detail the procedure for implementation. To help readers share the experience and excitement of encountering, secret wartime documents from a crisis point in our history, they have been rekeyed in Courier typeface, following the original styling and punctuation as closely as possible. The code is presented in order of priority as set out in the original document. To add context, I have included a timeline, and a brief introduction to each section.

N.S.W. STATE WAR EFFORT CO-ORDINATION COMMITTEE ORGANISATION

(With special reference to "Scorched Earth")

Local Army Command

NAVY
N.S Reg 45 d

CITIZENRY
N.S Reg 35 a

ARMY
N.S.Reg 37

Army Directive

N.S.W. STATE WAR EFFORT CO-ORDINATION COMMITTEE

SECRETARY

SCORCHED EARTH SUB-COMMITTEE
CHAIRMAN

S.E Codes
Categories
Conferences

WATERCRAFT PANEL

V.D.C. M.S.B. FISHERIES

Watercraft

Immobilisation (Non Essential)

Control (Essential)

S.E. SUPPORT SQUADS (WATERCRAFT)

DENIAL PREPARATIONS

Citizen Owners or Users

DENIAL OPERATIONS

Army Signal

GENERAL PANEL

FIRE BRIGADES

Industries

Citizen possessions

S.E. SUPPORT SQUADS (CITIZEN-INDUSTRAL)

DENIAL PREPARATIONS

Citizens and Industries

DENIAL OPERATIONS

DEPARTMENTS AND SERVICES

PUBLIC UTILITIES

S.E. SUPPORT SQUADS (DEPARTMENTAL)

DENIAL PREPARATIONS

DENIAL OPERATIONS

Army Signal

Naval Authority

THE WEATHER

Cloudy and clear with northerly winds, seen changing to a cool south westerly condition with showers, slight seas.

DAILY MIRROR

SYDNEY

SPECIAL EDITION

Registered at the General Post Office, Sydney for transmission by post as a newspaper

Telephones: Business—BW.241 (6 lines)
Telephones: Editorial—FL.061 (10 lines)
Telephones: Editorial—FL.061 (10 lines)

Vol. 1, No. 181   SYDNEY, MONDAY, DECEMBER 8, 1941   PRICE, 2d

JAPANESE ATTACK ON MALAYA AND HAWAII
GREAT NAVAL AND AIR BATTLES IN PROGRESS

From the Daily Mirror's Special Correspondent

WASHINGTON, Monday. — At 2.30 a.m. today, Australian time, Japanese warships and bombers attacked vital American bases in Hawaii and the Philippiines, 1870 miles north of Australia.

It is officially announced in Melbourne that the Japanese have also launched an attack on the borders of Thailand and British Malaya, on the Kra Isthmus, slightly on the British side of the border.

In a dramatic White House announcement it was stated that Pearl Harbor, great naval base on the main Hawaiian Island of Oahu, had been attacked.

President Roosevelt has ordered the immediate mobilisation of all naval, army and air force personnel throughout the United States.

A few minutes later came another announcement — Manila, main base in the Philippines was being attacked.

Several Jap. Bombers Shot Down

Great naval and air battles are raging around Pearl Harbor, the Hawaiian Schneider Airfield west of Honolulu, and at Manila.

One hundred and fifty Japanese planes are engaged in the attack on Pearl Harbor, and Honolulu reports that several have been shot down. Anti-aircraft guns at Pearl Harbor are in action, and clouds of smoke hang over the naval yard.

Correspondents in Hawaii radio telephoned the story to the United States, and the explosions could be clearly heard over 'phone.

The United States Army and Navy are carrying on under undisclosed orders designed for the protection of the United States.

The attack on Manila was heralded by the arrival of two Japanese planes over the city.

Naval Bombardment of Pearl Harbor

IMMEDIATELY following the appearance of planes over Pearl Harbor, a Japanese Warship appeared off the harbor and began a heavy bombardment.

Another message states that an American Army transport carrying lumber has been torpedoed 1300 miles from San Francisco.

Air reconnaissance by Catalina flying boats of the R.A.F. and planes of the R.A.A.F. revealed that after rounding Cambodia Point the convoy steamed north towards Thailand.

Mobilisation of British Imperial army, navy and air force personnel is going on at Singapore, and similar measures have been taken at Hongkong, where everything has been put on a war footing. The entire garrison, which is at a very high peak of efficiency, is ready for anything.

Japan's Naval & Army Strength—P. 4, Pictures P. 2 & 3

TIMELINE[1]

1941

7 December: Japanese aircraft stage surprise attack on US Fleet at Pearl Harbor, Hawaii, bringing the United States into World War II

8 December: Immediately prior to the attack on Pearl Harbor, Japanese troops land on the north-east coasts of Malaya and Thailand; United Kingdom declares war on Japan

9 December: Australia declares war on Japan

12 December: Australian men are called up for home defence service

12 December: A small Australian force is sent to support Dutch and Portuguese troops on Timor, 500 km from Australia

22 December: After the Japanese invasion of Luzon, US troops en route to the Philippines are diverted to Australia and arrive in Brisbane

25 December: Hong Kong surrenders to the Japanese

27 December: Australian Prime Minister John Curtin declares that Australia 'looks to America' for its defence

1942

January 1942: ABDA (American-British-Dutch-Australian) forces are ordered to hold the so-called Malay Barrier, from the Malay peninsula to the Dutch East Indies (Indonesia)

10 January: Japanese occupy Kuala Lumpur

19 January: British North Borneo surrenders to the Japanese

23 January: Japanese seize Rabaul, the capital of Australian-controlled New Guinea

24 January: War Cabinet begins discussing a 'scorched earth' policy in event of a Japanese invasion

25 January: Army Minister Frank Forde orders military commanders in all threatened areas to implement a scorched earth policy if local forces are forced to withdraw

27 January: NSW Forestry Commissioner E.H.F. Swain submits a 'scorched earth' proposal to NSW Premier William McKell

30 January: British and Commonwealth forces withdraw from Malaya to Singapore. Japanese troops land in Dutch East Indies. Japanese planes shoot down a Qantas flying boat en route from Darwin to Timor.

31 January: The Australian workforce is mobilised under Manpower Regulations, which conscript people to work in particular industries and occupations to assist the war effort

1 February: Australian and Dutch troops are captured by Japanese forces on Ambon, Dutch East Indies

3 February: Japanese aircraft make their first raid on Port Moresby

15 February: Allied forces in Singapore surrender to the Japanese; almost 15,000 Australians, mostly from 8th Division, are taken prisoner

16 February: Curtin refers to the coming 'Battle of Australia'. The Scorched Earth subcommittee of the NSW State War Effort Co-ordination Committee meets for the first time in Sydney under Swain's chairmanship

17 February: Curtin defies British Prime Minister Winston Churchill and stops Australian troops returning from the Middle East from being diverted to Burma

19 February: Japanese planes bomb Darwin; official death toll 243. Invasion is thought to be imminent. Between this date and November 1943, northern Australia is subjected to another 63 air raids, though most cause minimal or no damage

20–24 February: Japanese invade Timor

27 February: The NSW Scorched Earth subcommittee presents its initial report; details are to be refined over the next few weeks by industry and military experts

3 March: Japanese aircraft bomb Broome; 70–100 killed, 40 injured

9 March: Java surrenders to the Japanese

16 March: US General Douglas MacArthur, having fled the Philippines, arrives in Australia; one month later, MacArthur is formally appointed Supreme Allied Commander South-West Pacific Area. Some Australians find the US presence reassuring; others fear it will make Australia more of a target

6 April: The US 41st Infantry Division arrives in Australia

16 April: The NSW Scorched Earth subcommittee awaits military endorsement of draft denial codes for civilians and industry

4–8 May: The Battle of the Coral Sea prevents a Japanese landing at Port Moresby

29 May: At 3 am, a Japanese reconnaissance aircraft circles Sydney Harbour

31 May: Japanese mini-subs enter Sydney Harbour and are fired on by USS *Chicago*; 21 people are killed when a ferry is torpedoed at Garden Island

4–7 June: The US cripples Japanese naval power in the Battle of Midway, destroying four of Japan's six remaining aircraft carriers

8 June: Suburbs of Sydney and Newcastle are shelled by Japanese submarines

30 July: The War Cabinet issues a formal directive to guide planning for total denial of resources to the enemy and focusing on northern Australia

August 1942–February 1943: US and Japanese forces struggle on Guadalcanal; for the Japanese, this fight supersedes a planned attack on Port Moresby

17–25 September: Having reached ridges within sight of Port Moresby, Japanese forces on the Kokoda Trail are ordered to withdraw to New Guinea's north coast

23 November: The NSW government endorses a final Scorched Earth Code and associated policy documents.

1943

11 June: Curtin announces that Australia is no longer at risk of invasion

ABBREVIATIONS

AASC	Australian Army Service Corps
ARP	Air Raid Precautions
BIPOD	Bulk Issue Petrol and Oil Depot
Capt.	Captain
CCC	Citizen [also Civil] Collaboration Column
CCCC	Committee of Citizen Collaboration Columns
Col.	Colonel
Comds	Commands
COR	Commonwealth Oil Refinery
CSR Co.	Colonial Sugar Refinery Company
E in C	Engineer in Chief
HMA	His Majesty's Australian
HP	horsepower
HQ	headquarters
I&SCSN Co.	Illawarra & South Coast Steamship Navigation Company
Lt	lieutenant
L of C area	Line of Communication area, a military district
NCSN Co.	North Coast Steamship Navigation Company
NES	National Emergency Services
NRMA	National Roads and Motorists' Association
Ops	operations
PMG	Postmaster-General, Postmaster-General's Department
POL	petroleum, oil, lubricants
PWD	Public Works Department
QM	quartermaster
RAC(A)	Royal Automobile Club (of Australia)
RAE	Royal Australian Engineers
RAN	Royal Australian Navy
SESS	Scorched Earth Support Squad
SO	staff officer
SWECC	State War Effort Co-ordination Committee
VDC	Volunteer Defence Corps

Introduction

1942—IMPERILLED AUSTRALIA!

The devastating Japanese attack on the American naval base at Pearl Harbor, Hawaii, on 7 December 1941 marked the start of a long-anticipated conflict in the greater Pacific. The United States declared war on Japan; its allies Great Britain and Australia soon followed suit. As Japanese forces swept through Malaya and into the Philippines and Indonesia (then the Dutch East Indies), fears grew that they would also invade Australia.[1] Although Japanese commanders did discuss such a move in early 1942, they decided to focus first on securing the resource-rich islands to Australia's north and then to isolate Australia by capturing New Caledonia, Fiji and other islands in the Pacific.

Australians, of course, were not privy to Japanese plans. To them, an invasion appeared all too likely. Given the stunning speed of Japanese advances, failing to prepare for an invasion would have been foolish. That belief was reinforced when Japan seized the British naval bastion of Singapore in February 1942, sinking two British warships and capturing 118,000 British, Indian and Australian troops. Over the next several months, fears of invasion surged as Japanese aircraft bombed Darwin, Broome and Townsville,

mini-subs entered Sydney Harbour, and the eastern suburbs of
Sydney and Newcastle were shelled by submarines lying offshore.
The immense length of Australia's coastline and the fact that most
of the country's troops were serving overseas convinced many
people that if an invasion was indeed being planned, preventing it
would be impossible.

Wherever the Japanese invaded Asia, they plundered local
resources from forests to oil fields and used locals and captured
troops as slave labour. The Curtin government was determined
that this would never happen in Australia. It advocated a scorched
earth policy that would deprive the enemy of every resource that
might aid its war effort. The initial focus was on military assets,
such as air strips, munitions dumps and fuel depots, but the policy
was soon extended to civil resources. By early 1942, the government had asked the states to draw up 'Scorched Earth' schemes
(the name was later toned down to 'Denial of Resources to the
Enemy') to come into effect in the event of an invasion.[2] These
plans did not signal defeatism. John Curtin assured state Premiers
they were 'part of the general defence scheme and are not in any
way inconsistent with the government's resolve to defend Australia
to the limit of our capacity'.[3]

In making their preparations, the states were to keep in mind
that—as the New South Wales code put it—'There is plenty
of Australia from which we could evacuate without danger of
defeat . . . There are places in Australia from which we must not
retreat. These are Sydney and Newcastle, Melbourne, Brisbane
and Canberra.' Each state was divided into rural areas that could
be abandoned to an advancing enemy, and urban and industrial
centres to be held at all costs. If rural and remote areas were
attacked or occupied, their residents would evacuate in stages to
ever larger towns. In their wake, 'a TOTAL denial policy will be
implemented, i.e., the complete and total removal or destruction
of everything likely to maintain or assist the enemy in his
operations'. In the 'fortress' cities, however, there would be no
evacuation. Here, 'a PARTIAL denial policy will be implemented,
i.e., certain essential services to enable the population to live will

be left intact, together with food supplies. All other services, utilities, vehicles, materials and everything likely to be of assistance to the enemy in his operations will be removed to a safe area or totally destroyed.'[4] Denial was not to be compromised by a desire to recover resources later, since the enemy 'will almost certainly himself destroy anything of value in his retreat'.[5]

All states prepared evacuation and denial plans, but the NSW Code was the first and the most comprehensive. This was partly because the state held almost half the country's population,[6] its largest harbour and many of its most valuable resources—and partly because of the energy of Premier William McKell and his Scorched Earth point man, E.H.F. (Harold) Swain. In late January 1942, Swain, the state Forestry Commissioner, submitted to McKell a document titled 'Total War! . . . And Total Citizen Collaboration' (reproduced in Chapter 1). Impressed, McKell asked Swain to establish and chair a subcommittee of the NSW State War Effort Co-ordination Committee; its job would be to plan a scorched earth policy for the state in line with the Commonwealth's recent directive.[7] The subcommittee had two other members: Police Inspector A.H. Standen, and Colonel J.J.L. McCall, representing the Base Commandant, Eastern Command.[8] Their first meetings were held on 16 and 17 February 1942.

On 19 February, Darwin was attacked by 188 Japanese aircraft. The official death count was 243, though it was almost certainly higher than that.[9] It was widely believed that an invasion of northern Australia was only weeks away, and that an invasion of the east coast would follow. Worried citizens began preparing for a fight. The Volunteer Defence Corps, a part-time 'home guard' force, extended membership to men in reserved occupations, who had previously been exempt or barred from military enlistment. By December 1942, the VDC had 100,000 men. They focused on their local areas, protecting key installations and preparing roadblocks. They trained in marksmanship and guerrilla tactics, often with improvised weapons. Civilians around the country acted as volunteer air observers and practised air raid precautions. In Ku-ring-gai shire, north of Sydney, over a thousand residents formed a 'People's Army' and trained in guerrilla tactics. The popular novelist Ion Idriess, a World War I veteran and an early advocate of such training, wrote a series of manuals called *The Australian Guerrilla*, with titles like *Shoot to Kill*, *Guerrilla Tactics* and *Trapping the Jap*.[10]

Impelled by the mounting public alarm, Swain's subcommittee completed a basic Scorched Earth Code (reproduced as Chapter 2) in just six weeks. Its aims were:

- To prevent the enemy living on the country, and using our property against us.
- To force him to use his own precious shipping. To deplete his own country of supplies, to sustain and maintain his own armies.
- To attack him, through fire and destruction.
- To obstruct and to impede him, and dislodge his foothold.
- To slow up his advance.
- To leave him nothing to loot and remove to his own country.
- To deny him everything in our country.

The Code assumed that civilians would be evacuated in stages from the most vulnerable areas (or those the Army had abandoned) to areas where the Army was still in control. Women with young children and the very old and ill could move to 'fortress' areas immediately, but others should continue living and working as normal, leaving only on orders from the Army.

As an area was evacuated, its key resources would be disabled or destroyed. The Code identified all such resources, their locations, the best methods for their destruction, and the authorities responsible for destroying them. It recommended that special Scorched Earth Support Squads be set up to instruct civilians in the Code and help them prepare for evacuation and dispose of property such as boats, vehicles and tools (Chapter 12). The first squads were established and in training by mid-April 1942.[11]

Despite its name, the Code regarded total devastation as a last-ditch measure to be used only in dire emergency. As Swain wrote: 'This policy is called "scorched earth", although normally the denial will be selective rather than devastative . . . the denial command will be issued by the Army only if danger is imminent and enemy pressure critical.' Denial would take place in stages: first 'tactical demolition—jetties, bridges, railways, roads and telegraph', then 'parched earth destruction—oil wells and supplies, coastal craft, motor vehicles and foodstuffs'. The 'third degree' was 'scorched earth destruction', which 'extends to everything!'

Various government departments were asked to develop scorched earth strategies—the Mines Department prepared one for coal mines; Main Roads helped the Army with evacuation plans and road construction; the Department of Road Transport prepared a memorandum on petrol and oil destruction; Public Works and the Maritime Services Board devised a strategy for wharves and jetties; Agriculture set up a Primary Industries Evacuation committee and prepared denial plans for stock and crops; the Maritime Services Board and Fisheries advised the Navy on watercraft; and Forestry looked at timber supply.

An important principle of the Commonwealth scorched earth policy was that in the event of an invasion the entire nation would be mobilised. Every citizen and worker would have a part to play. Many of the scorched earth measures depended on individuals sharing their local knowledge and expertise, and putting the collective defence ahead of private interests. Sacrifices would have to be made if the invaders were to be repelled. As Swain declared: 'in Total War—the War for Survival—the citizen is no longer a detached neutral or a chattel, but the involved majority, deeply concerned in events and for victory'.

Over a thousand people in Ku-ring-gai Shire were in training in the
Citizens' Guerrilla Force. Pictured are members of the Turramurra Force.

1

TOTAL WAR—AND TOTAL CITIZEN COLLABORATION

Harold Swain, the chairman of the Scorched Earth subcommittee, was appointed not so much because of his professional background (he was New South Wales Forestry Commissioner in 1942), but because of his force of character, his prodigious organisational ability, and his passion for the cause of civil defence. His entry in the *Australian Dictionary of Biography* makes no reference to his role in developing the Scorched Earth Code, but it notes that he was an ardent advocate of forests who was confident in his own opinions and impatient with those who disagreed.[1] A tribute by Peter Holzworth noted that Swain 'had an ego the size of the Melbourne Cricket Ground . . . His stoushes were legendary! . . . he was right and everybody else was wrong.' But staff and bush friends admired him for his defence of forests and forestry.[2]

In the document he sent to Premier William McKell in January 1942 (reproduced in this chapter), Swain asserted that 'no part of our coasts can be regarded as immune from bombings, shellings or actual landings'. He went on to detail what would likely follow such

1

landings, invoking the examples of Korea, Manchuria, China, the
Philippines and Malaya. Australians, he said, had to be prepared
for invasion and its horrific consequences; the Japanese would
make no distinction between soldiers and civilians. That meant
civilians must collaborate closely with the military in a 'defence-
in-depth' that could only succeed if the entire population was
thoroughly prepared: informed, trained and organised. Every last
man and woman must be part of the war effort, from soldiers
and militiamen to police officers, stockmen, doctors, taxi drivers,
firefighters, engineers, boot makers, carrier pigeon owners and
cooks. All belonged, in his scheme, to one of the 'Ten National
Emergency Services', which must stand ready to fight 'with tin
helmet, gas mask and rifle (or grenade, or butcher's knife or club)
at the ready'.

He envisaged that while the armed forces engaged in battle,
civilian guerrillas would assist them from the rear, supplying them
with food and intelligence, serving as scouts and messengers,
manning tank traps and roadblocks. These guerrilla bushrangers
could live 'aboriginally' on rabbits, birds and game, fish and eels
and boiled kurrajong roots, and improvise their own weapons—
'an ironbark spike might do as much damage as a bayonet'.

Swain assessed and identified evacuation routes from the coast
to the interior. He drew up 'battle orders' for civilians, who would
be formed into 'Civilian Collaboration Columns'. These orders
included digging air-raid shelters, watching potential enemy
landing places, keeping cars filled with fuel, making identification
discs and preparing an evacuation kit. Specific instructions were
added for workers and business owners: grocers were to prepare
stocks of flour, sugar, tobacco and soap; farmers would ready
horse carts for use in an evacuation; blacksmiths would make
hand grenade containers; cooks and waitresses would establish
mobile canteens.

In Swain's all-encompassing vision, no adult citizen was
exempt, and none was unimportant. 'EVERYONE must be used,' he
wrote. And there was no time to waste: 'Every citizen will get
busy at once.'

26.1.42.

TOTAL WAR - AND TOTAL CITIZEN COLLABORATION

ø/ RECONNAISSANCE!

Australia is the British arsenal of the East; and a Pacific bastion on the southern route between U.S.A. and Japan.

It becomes therefore of considerable military interest to Japan - and no part of our coasts can be regarded as immune from bombings, shellings, or actual landings.

The invasion method will most likely be initial infiltration at many points, using our own fishing boats and launches to swarm up and down the coast, projecting spearheads through ascertained lines of weakness, spreading through the forests, scattering points of entry like sparks from a bush fire, advancing by looting, creating confusion and stampede, using our own people against us, converging upon the core of resistance in the industrial concentrations of our cities.

Our answer must be to counter every inch of the way - with the entire population mobilised as one army of essential war functioning, with every unit knowing his or her battle duty.

We must delay, delay, DELAY - knowing that help will come.

There must be no evacuation - as such; but no Australian - and no alien - must fall into enemy hands; and there must be neither water, food, nor supply in this country for the Japanese.

Total war is unbridled license: and complete spoilation.

Massacre, torture, ransom, pillaging, vice

monopolies, and all types of racketeering are features
of the Japanese concept of making the occupied
country pay for the upkeep of the Japanese army and
gendarmerie, to build up the private fortunes of
its army chiefs and to provide pleasant looting for
the peasant soldier. Women become chattels and the
victims of unspeakable beastliness; men the slaves.
The Japanese humor will sometimes pay for services
rendered - in Australian notes printed in Tokio.

This is authenticated.

What has happened in Korea, Manchuria and China
is being repeated in Malaya and the Philippines.
Even in Russia the technique of the German forces is
identical. Witness - the Russian official category.

Further, the Japanese will not forget the White
Australia policy!

We are assured by authority that these things will
happen here at any moment; as to the where we have
no inkling.

Planning for citizen collaboration-at-war suffers
the lag resulting from unbelief in the incredible;
it remains for the planner, even against his own
incredibility, to labor at a plan so decentralised,
self-starting and all-encompassing, that it
becomes an automatically acceptable control and
guide to every person at the sudden moment when the
incredible becomes horrified belief, and imminent
stampede, and the enemy's aim of civil confusion is
precipitated upon our defending forces.

Witness what happened at Penang - where incredible
civilian incredibility resulted in disaster.

The military plan must apportion the civilian
operation.

This war is not a war confined politely to
opposing armies, with civilians as harmless and
unharmed observers.

Uniform or no uniform - and of the Japanese
soldiery in Malaya only 50% wore uniforms - the
entire civilian population is in World War II
equally with its soldiery.

The passing of war conventions must be believed.
We have seen that the declaration of an open city
has lost its old-time value. We know that civil
populations will be enslaved to manufacture
munitions for the slaughter of their own kith
and kin.

Only raw realism can energise us to the realism
of total war. It is just plain Horror and Murder.
And as we expect no mercy let us as civilians, even
though unarmed, slaughter the armed "yellow dwarfs"
with our own "tooth and claw" in our own familiar
forests.

Wintringham[3] has told us what was accomplished in
Spain by civilians.

At least we can outnumber the potential invading
force.

ø/ NOT EVACUATION BUT DEFENCE-IN-DEPTH - WITH TOTAL
CITIZEN COLLABORATION IN A MASTER PLAN.

There have been, in the dim past of a week or two
ago advocates of the policies both of "staying-put"
and of "evacuation".

Wholesale evacuation in emergency of helpless
civilian communities inland would cast impossible
tasks upon a transport system weakened by petrol
shortage; it would block the roads and hinder our
fighting men in their life and death efforts; it
would create impossible supply chaos behind the
lines, and burden an unorganised water supply
after a seven year drought; it would initiate
disorganisation and a defeatist morale.

It would suit the enemy.

There are 2,700,000 people in New South Wales, most of them on the coast; and more than half of them in the hundred odd air miles between Kembla and Newcastle.

We cannot evacuate from our Moscow and Leningrad - our cores of war production.

Nor can we quite "stay-put" - as if at our peace-time stations.

The policy of "staying-put" would leave a vast civil population passive and unhelpful in the way of our armies of production and defence; in the hands of the enemy this inert mass would become a hostage and would be used as such mercilessly by the Japanese soldiery.

Our plan must be one neither of evacuation nor of staying-put; but one of organised military-civil defence-in-depth, in which the civil population becomes part of our war organisation within a MASTER PLAN for Total Citizen Collaboration in Total War.

That total citizen collaboration is indispensable to victories is obvious upon reflection of the consequences of its complete absence in France and of its inadequacy in Malaya.

Civil collaboration commenced in the Philippines when Filipino drivers smashed the cylinder heads of their motor buses rather than that the Japanese should requisition them for the conveyance of troops.

In China, civil collaboration is called banditry - by the Japanese! In Russia it is called guerilla warfare, and was organised by a complete code.

But plain citizens have many opportunities in war other than to take the available rifles out of the hands of their mates in uniform.

In total war uniforms are of reduced significance - 50% of the Japanese soldiery in Malaya wore coolie disguises!

In Malaya the Japanese were preceded by
requisition parties which collected food, clothing,
shoes, petrol, bicycles, cars, buses, and loot and
commandeered boats for coastwise infiltrations.

The plain citizen can see to it that such things
do not happen here. But he needs to be organised to
learn his part.

Whilst the Army Chiefs in Australia are hard
put to it to improvise a fighting force from raw
recruits, it becomes a duty of civil Government to
complete our citizen collaboration-at-war - and to
plan it to the last dot of perfection.

The Germans had ten years to work out such a plan:
the Japanese have had since 1915, at least.

We have a day or a week, or a month perhaps.-

- And every succeeding moment will alter our
attitude to this Plan until we are projected on to
the ultimate -

Until then every edition of a Master Plan will be
out of date immediately it is drafted: but redrafts
must flow continuously until the ultimate, the while
implementation proceeds, and ordinarily sequential
processes telescope.

There needs to be an Editor-in-chief of the Master
Plan who will incorporate and order the Sectional
drafts of the specialist sub-editors as fast as they
develop.

Everything must be fit and time.

To state a problem is to solve it.

This problem is ramified to the nth degree.

Those who have to state it will have the most
arduous task in laboured thinking ever given to
Australians to be done on time - but it will save a
situation and build a new one in record time.

For Defence-in-depth, there must be an instant
acceleration of peace-time decentralisation

policies! This in itself is a colossal duty,
involving transfers of industry, but it is an
integral factor of strategy.

Necessity compels a straight relation to emergency,
with every Australian accommodated at the essential
post for which his peace time functioning fits him,
knowing his job and ready to march.

Vague and purposeless self-activity will not
suffice!

ø/ BATTLE STATIONS FOR ALL - THE TEN NATIONAL
EMERGENCY SERVICES

A modern civilisation is complex and cannot be
reduced in modern war to the simple elements of
a tribal war, viz (i) fighting men; (ii) serving
women.

The Minister for the War Organisation of Industry[4]
has told us that there is no such thing as a non-
essential industry.

Our military text books did not contemplate the
incorporation of this complex civilisation in a
fighting-supplying-marching army of the whole.

The German and Japanese did!

Before we can marshall it to war, we must know
and accept its components and guard ourselves
against the elemental temptation to revert to tribal
simplicity.

This is the purpose of Man Power Policy.

One fighting man requires seven working men
behind him.

The principal battle stations of a war of 1942 -
the ten actual National Emergency Services - are:

1. The Fighting Forces - the A.I.F., R.A.A.F. and
   Militia - up to our capacity to modernly equip
   them!

2. <u>Civil Administration-at-War</u>: Implementing the Master Plan, and its Local Action detail.

   The Police, Justice, Law, the Church, Banking and Finance, Forestry, Stock, Agriculture and other Government Departments functioning at war, Schools (children protection and supervision), Councils and Essential Services (Gas and Electricity regeneration and supply, water supply, sewerage and drainage) and so on - with their requisite clerical and accounting staffs.

3. <u>Auxiliary Defence</u>:
   (i)   <u>The Volunteer Defence Corps</u>: - Attested volunteers over military age or in reserved occupations, who drill and may fight as a section of the militia.

   (ii)   <u>Guerilla groups</u>: Self active unattested men (and boys and women) who practice guerilla exercises, street fighting, obstruction etc.

   (iii) <u>Town fire brigades; A.R.P. (N.E.S.) Organisation; Bush Fire Brigades</u> — The latter manned by men who often have essential occupations to maintain at war, but who function in invasion against incendiarism, bombings and shellings.

   (iv)   <u>Labor Corps</u>: Men, (and women) from both essential and non-essential industries, who in the course of invasion or war changes become detached from industry and become available, through National Service offices, as a pool from which can be drawn either reinforcements for the fighting forces, or labor for trench-digging, fortifications, bush firefighting, demolition, supply, the transfer of industry and so on.

(v)   Friendly aliens, or even prisoners-of-war
        may be organised within this group.

(vi)   <u>Ambulances and Hospitals</u> - including
        convalescent homes and mental hospitals
        with Doctors, Dentists, Opticians,
        Druggists, X-ray Operators, Undertakers,
        Cemetery Staffs, Artificial Limb Makers,
        Surgical Supplies, Red Cross, First Aid
        etc.

4. <u>Transport Services</u>:
   (i)   Shipping and ferries (plus pilot services,
           harbour works and light houses services,
           hire launches and fishing boats).
   (ii)   Air transport.
   (iii)   Railways and tramways.
   (iv)   Road transport:
           (a) Cartage contractors and taxi-cabs.
           (b) Auxiliary road transport.
           (c) N.R.M.A., R.A.C.
           (d) Garages and Service Stations.
           (e) Oil depots.
   (v)   Ship and boat builders.

5. <u>Communication and News Services</u>:
   (i)   Beam, cable and wireless.
   (ii)   Post and telegraph.
   (iii)   Radio Stations.
   (iv)   Newspapers.
   (v)   Printing, engraving, photography.
   (vi)   Messenger services.
   (vii)   Carrier pigeon owners.
   (viii) Auxiliaries.

6. <u>Commissariat</u>:
   (1) <u>Services</u>:
       Canteens; hotels, restaurants, cafes, ham
       and beef shops, railway refreshment rooms,

bakers, fishmongers, fruiterers, butchers, grocers, cooks, waitresses - all and more would be needed when homes are disrupted.

(2) Primary production and processing:

    (a) Cattle and stock: dairying: sheep stations.

    (b) Wheat farmers.

    (c) Fishermen.

    (d) Sugar growing and refining.

    (e) Tobacco production and manufacture.

    (f) Abattoirs.

    (g) Butter, cheese and milk factories and services.

    (h) Flourmills.

    (i) Food processing, preservation, canning, margarine, salt manufacture.

    (j) Refrigeration and dehydration.

    (k) Containers, bags and cases.

7. Engineering Service-at-war:

    (i)   Engineers and draftsmen.

    (ii)   Mechanics, blacksmiths and farriers.

    (iii) Plumbers, locksmiths, tinsmiths, copper and brass workers.

    (iv)   Galvanisers, lead and shot, wire rope, cable, fence and barbed wire.

    (v)   Shovel, spade and pick manufacturers and tool handles.

    (vi)   Scientific instruments and appliance makers.

    (vii) Carriage and body, cycle and motor builders.

    (viii) Road-making, farm tractors.

8. War-time Building Construction and Repairs

    (i)   Architects, carpenters, joiners.

    (ii)   Concrete and brick.

(iii)   Paint and varnish - painters.

(iv)   Artists and camouflage.

9. Basic Materials and Services:

(i)   Coal.

(ii)   Metals and minerals: cement and lime: quarries.

(iii)   Timber (forestry, timber supply, sawmills, timber getters, wood workers, charcoal burners, case making and cooperage, match making, airplane supply etc.)

(iv)   Leather (tan barks, tanners, leather trades and boot makers).

(v)   Textiles etc. (uniforms and essential clothing, wool and cotton mills, water proof and gas proof materials, parachute silks, tent, sail and canvas, bags, dye works).

(vi)   Rubber - motor tyres and rubber goods.

(vii)   Oil, shale and power alcohol: lubricating oils (castor oil planting).

(viii) Cordage, ropes and twine.

(ix)   Paper and pulp.

(x)   Paints.

(xi)   Drugs and chemicals.

10. Munitions and War Supplies:

(i)   Aircraft production.

(ii)   Munition and armament factories.

(iii)   Explosives: oil refining and distribution.

(iv)   Ship building.

In the Netherlands East Indies, the Dutchman daily arrives at his work with tin helmet, gas mask and rifle, ready for Invasion Drill from 4 p.m. to 7 p.m. - or for invasion itself.

Working and fighting are one and the same in this
war for the earth.

In production lies our Fighting Strength.

We must do both!

The Ten National Emergency Services must be kept
going though battles rage - but with tin helmet, gas
mask and rifle (or grenade, or butcher's knife or
club) at the ready.

And ready to march as Citizen Collaboration
Columns, with industries and accoutrements
complete.

The public is now war conscious, uneasy, both
urging and bewildered by urgings, breaking often
into vague self-activity leaving essential jobs
under emotional stress, asking for battle stations.

It must be given battle stations.

And EVERYONE must be used.

We have to learn how to depute, delegate, and
ramify to the uttermost individual.

But the individual must feel in himself that he is
freely in his right place, so that he can function
with the energy of conviction.

Compulsion will be for the few.

We must start from the basis of <u>reshaping</u>
the civil structure - not disordering it, not
disintegrating it.

Work must continue and must accelerate; with
a pruning of civil and private development, a
disappearance of luxury goods, a reduction to the
stark essential, a focussing on the laborious
planned building of eventual victory through a new
rationalisation of every essential energy, a new
decentralisation.

- According to the Master Plan.

ø/ THE RURAL COAST - ITS ROUTES AND TERRAIN

There are two essentially different sectors of
our coast:
1. The Rural Coasts, North and South.
2. The Industrial Urban Concentration of
    Newcastle-Sydney-Port Kembla.

It is to be assumed that both will be the scene
of air bombings and shellings, and the first
of landings, enemy infiltration, assembly and
convergence on the second with attempts at outflanking by inland detour.

- And that, whilst our fighting forces give battle,
our civilian forces will withdraw to the forests
on the flanks, leaving behind neither hostage,
water, sustenance nor oil for the enemy, maintaining
themselves as Civil Collaboration Columns, supplying
and reinforcing our soldiers, scouting, guiding,
requisitioning, tank-trapping, giving total and
conforming support to the military plan, and keeping
open lines of communication inland, whilst blocking
the enemy in the bottlenecks of the mountain highways
and in the cul de sacs of the forests.

The accompanying map of N.S.W. illustrates the
coastal routes and terrain, viz:
1. State Highways.
2. Main Roads.
3. Subsidiary Roads.
4. Bad bottlenecks.
5. Impassable country.
6. Cul de sacs.
7. Refugee centers.
8. Railways.
9. Dangerous outlet routes from coast to inland.
10. Coastal outlet routes recommended.

Along the whole length of the N.S.W. coast there
are seven State Highways and eleven Main Roads
leading from the sea to inland.

Otherwise there are no subsidiary roads capable
of carrying wheeled traffic across the coastal
escarpment.

There are tracks which can be used by bushmen on
horse or afoot.

Most of the State Highways or Main Roads in
question possess bad bottlenecks where traffic
jams can cause disaster, or conversely provide
defensive and delaying positions and road blocks.
The approximate positions of those bottlenecks are
shown in red on the routes marked on the map.

The bottlenecks consist mostly of steep winding
grades, especially on the slopes of the Main
Dividing Range. In other places the roads lead
through narrow, deep river gorges.

From the Queensland border south to Camden Haven,
the mean distance from the coast to the eastern edge
of the tablelands is in an air line about 60 miles,
and the time needed for withdrawal in average 20
mile daily stages is generally four to six days by
road. As most of the routes are along river valleys,
water is plentiful - against this, water supplies
cannot be withheld from an enemy.

Interposed between those routes (further
particulars of which are given hereunder) are areas
of impassable country, in many instances terminating
in cul de sacs from which retiring civilians or
advancing enemy would find extrication almost
impossible, and the former event must be carefully
avoided. All population must be drained northerly
and southerly to the most convenient of the outlet
roads.

Of all the outlet routes from the coast to the
inland, four State Highways numbered on the map (1),
(9), (12) and (13) are the most easily traversed and
the most difficult to defend, and with the exception

Queensland

Bourke

Darling River

Cabar

Broken Hill

South Australia

Hay

Murray

Deniliquin

Victoria

River

NEW SOUTH WALES

COASTAL ROUTES & TERRAIN for DEFENCE in DEPTH

Forestry Commission of N.S.W.

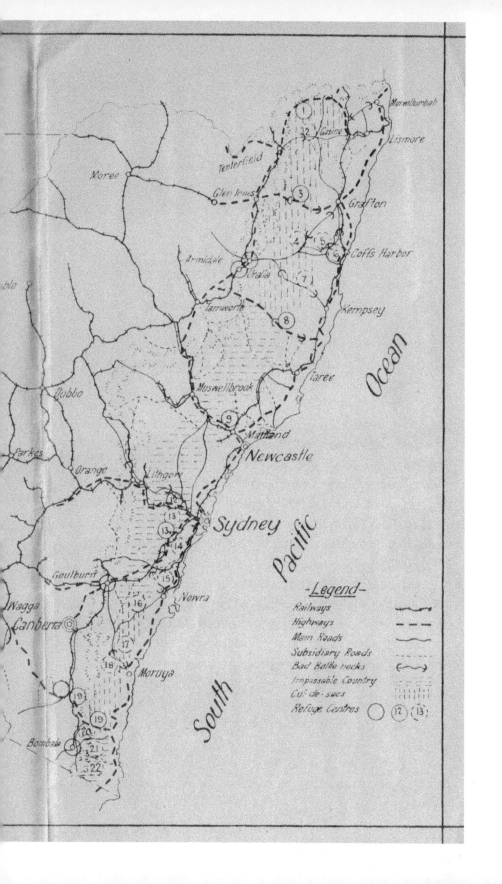

of No. (12) all of them could be by-passed by an
advancing enemy.

These danger routes are in order of numbering,
north to south:

(1) New England Highway where it parallels the
     Queensland border and the Main Road Extension
     leading from it to Kyogle-Casino.
(9) New England Highway leading from Newcastle
     through the Hunter Valley.
(12) Great Western Highway leading westerly from
     Sydney.
(13) Hume Highway leading south-westerly from
     Sydney.

Special measures will be needed to safe-guard
retirement along these routes; also for their
defence.

No. 1 is a circuitous route and should be availed of
for the retirement of those civilians inhabiting the
immediately adjacent country.

The general retirement for the Tweed-Lismore-
Casino area and for the Upper Clarence River Valley,
should be via Main Road No. 8 on map and which leads
westerly from Casino over the Richmond Range and
through Tabulam and Drake to Tenterfield.

Good main and developmental roads intersect this
route in a north and south direction in the Richmond
and Clarence Valleys, and these will easily serve
to drain the population of this portion of the State
and lead then to the western outlet along No. 8.

No. 2 Route: Retirement from Casino to Tenterfield
or vicinity would occupy about five days, traversing
20 miles average per day.

First day retire to Theresa Creek or Shannon
Brook, good travelling through cleared country.

Water usually available in creeks; envelopment by enemy easily achieved on this stage. About 16 miles.

Second day – cross Richmond Range and camp on west of river at Tabulam. Abundant water in river. Enemy could be delayed on Richmond Range slopes. Mostly clear country will be traversed. About 18 miles.

Third day – to Cataract River, Sandy Hills, traverse much timber country – Girard State Forest. Long stage – 27 miles. Abundant water.

Fourth day – climb range, destroy road up ascent and camp on river near Tenterfield. About 14 or 15 miles.

No. 3 Route – State Highway, Grafton to Glen Innes:
First day – Chambigne Creek Water. Nine miles. Camp in timber. Abundant water. Mostly clear country traversed.

Second day – camp at Buccarumbi. Abundant water. Timbered and cleared country traversed. About 18 miles.

Third day – along very winding, narrow River Road to Sheep Station Creek. Timbered and open. Abundant water. About 20 miles; block road.

Fourth day – to about Bruisers Creek. Mixed country, still in valleys. About 16 miles.

Fifth day – to Mann River. Abundant water, mixed country. About 17 miles.

Sixth day – climb Big Hill. Camp about Bald Knob. Sabotage road Big Hill.

No. 4 Route – Grafton to Ebor:
First day – Blaxlands or Coolang Creek, through open country. Twenty miles. Abundant water. Otherwise Nymboida River, 29 miles.

Second day – to Clouds Creek, mostly climbing and through timber. Water. 23 miles, or Billys Creek 23 miles.

Third day - Little Falls Creek (on Tableland) -
sabotage cuttings.

No. 5 Route - Coffs Harbour to Ebor:

First day - to Coramba, water abundant. Clear
country, 15 miles.

Second day - Coramba to Brooklana, mountain
road, abundant water. Twenty miles. Sabotage 7 mile
mountain road.

Third day - to Dorrigo. Narrow, winding roads,
easily blocked, or via Cascade deviation. Forest
road, 22 miles. Abundant water.

Fourth day - Middle Creek top, 23 miles. Mountain
roads, abundant water.

No. 6 Route - Raleigh-Dorrigo Tableland

1st day Bellingen by open road - 12 miles
2nd day to Dorrigo - steep mountain blockade -
   20 miles.
3rd day to Middle Creek - 23 miles.

No. 7 Route - Kempsey to Tableland:

1st day Hickey Creek - 17 miles.
2nd day Bellbrook - 16 miles.
3rd day Lagoon Creek - 16 miles.
4th day foot of Big Hill - 18 miles.
5th day to Styx or Jeogla tops.

Abundant water throughout and almost the whole
length of road can be blockaded through narrow
cuttings and steep grades. Much timbered country.

No. 8 Route - Port Macquarie to Tableland:

1st day to about Gannons Creek - 20 miles easy
   country.
2nd day Yarras Creek - 23 miles blockade roads.
3rd day Sawmill   - 23 miles   "   "

4th day Yarrowitch Tops - 23 miles "   "
Water abundant throughout - much road easily
    blocked.

Nos. 9 & 10 Routes:
    Must follow main roads. Sufficient water will be a
problem at present. Newcastle area.

Nos. 11, 12 & 13 Routes:
    Would be dealt with under evacuation from
Metropolitan area plans.

No. 14 Route - Albion Park to Moss Vale:
    1st day Robertson - 17 miles. Block mountain
        road.
    2nd day to Moss Vale.

No. 15 Route - Nowra to Moss Vale:
    1st day Kangaroo Valley. Water. 15 miles.
    2nd day Moss Vale - 21 miles. Sabotage mountain
        road.

No. 16 Route - Nowra to Braidwood:
    1st day Poor water.
    2nd day Nerriga. Sabotage cuttings - 43 miles.
    3rd day Charleyong - 20 miles. Water available.
    4th day Braidwood - 15 miles.

No. 17 Route - Bateman's Bay to Braidwood:
    1st day foot or top of Clyde Mountain, vicinity
        Monga. Water bad to this point, except for
        small splashes over roadway. About 25 miles.
    2nd day Braidwood - total 41 miles. Blockade
        mountain.

No. 18 Route - Moruya to Braidwood:
 1st day to Burrundulla - 20 miles. Water
  abundant.
 2nd day - Araluen. Blockade cuttings on river.
 3rd day - Braidwood. Blockade mountain road.

No. 19 Route - Bega to Nimmitabel (Brown Mountain
Road).
 1st day Bemboka. Winding road open country - 22
  miles.
 2nd day - top of mountain - sabotage road.
 3rd day - Nimmitabel - 26 miles.

No. 20 Route - Bega to Bombala:
 1st day - to foot of Tantawanglo Mountain -
  20 miles.
 2nd day - to Cathcart - 19 miles.
 3rd day - to Bombala - 11 miles.
 Total about 50 miles.

No. 21 Route, Pambula to Bombala, and Eden to
Bombala:
 (a) Pambula-Bombala (about 52 miles).
  1st day - to Wyndham - 19 miles.
  2nd day - to Cathcart - 22 miles.
  3rd day - to Bombala - 11 miles.
 (b) Eden-Bombala (about 58½ miles).
  1st day - to Burragate - 25 miles.
  2nd day - to Cathcart - 22½ miles
  3rd day - to Bombala - 11 miles.

 Further details of each route can be obtained
from the Forest Officer whose area is concerned.
 Details of all subsidiary draining roads leading
to them can also be furnished.

Emergency road construction required:

A glance at the map indicates that the Manning River Valley, with important centres of population like Taree, is the worst served area on the coast for a retirement to the highlands, no trafficable road existing.

A road up this valley would serve the population from as far south as Stroud.

Two road outlets should be constructed to this valley, firstly the missing link from about Knorritt Flat to Nowendoc, about 30 miles, which would give direct outlet from Taree and Wingham to Walcha. There already exists fair shire roads from Walcha to Nowendoc, and from Wingham to Knorritt Flat.

This road could serve the Nowendoc forests and could probably be extended to serve the Hanging Rock forests.

The second road should lead from Gloucester up the main Manning River basin and linking with a road up the Upper Hunter River, and so inland.

A road linking the Bulga Plateau with the Oxley Highway, via Doyles River, would also be advantageous.

ø/ BATTLE ORDERS FOR THE PLAIN CITIZEN ON THE RURAL COAST - A CITIZEN COLLABORATION CODE:

The Plain Citizen will function-at-war, in this war, in four essential roles, viz:-

  1. As a Private person.
  2. In Business.
  3. As Amateur Combatants.
  4. In Civil Collaboration Columns

and in two stages - which telescope in emergency; viz:

  1. Before battle.
  2. During battle.

In England in January, 1942, two British Field
Security police, wearing German uniforms and talking
German and broken English:
- ø/ Mixed with the London public without the
      slightest obstruction.
- ø/ Obtained important information from an
      R.A.F. flight lieutenant and an Army Officer.
- ø/ Borrowed cigarettes from a civilian.
- ø/ Had tea in the best German manner in the most
      popular cafe.
- ø/ Were not challenged by the Plain Citizen.

This war is the Plain Citizen's business!

These are the Plain Citizen's Battle Orders for
the Rural Coast of N.S.W.:-

Battle Orders for the Plain Citizen - (i) As a
private person:

1. Every citizen will at once complete Air Raid
   Precautions for his home and business, viz:
   (i)   Complete blackout and anti-shatter his
          windows.
   (ii)   Provide himself with bomb shovel and rake
          and water receptacles filled for both fire
          extinction and drinking purposes.
   (iii) Fire spotting.
   (iv)   Provide his own air raid shelter or dig a
          sawtooth slit trench in his back yard.
   (v)   Provide a supply of non-perishable food in
          the home.
2. Every citizen will refrain from lighting camp
   fires, loose fires, burning-off; and be
   responsible for the immediate extinction of any
   outbreak on his land, and to his neighbours for
   assistance in similar case.
3. Every citizen will economise in expenditure;
   purchase no luxury goods or non-essentials;

refrain from hoarding essentials, suspend
development - and salvage aluminium, rubber,
twine, rope, bags ...

4. Every citizen will parcel his personal
    valuables, documents (birth and marriage
    certificates, deeds, scrip &c.) maps and luxury
    goods - and lodge them in a place of safety
    inland if possible, and destroy maps - no map,
    even an ordinary tourist, advertising or railway
    map, must fall into enemy hands.

5. Every citizen will note the presence and
    movements of any suspicious alien stranger -
    German, Japanese, Italian, Finn, Thailander,
    ... and let it not be said that the enemy or the
    Fifth Column can bluff the Plain Citizen from his
    personal responsibility. Report to the Police.

6. Every citizen in his area will locate and keep
    watch on all potential landing places from air
    or sea - and learn to identify aeroplanes -
    particularly Japanese. He will immediately
    supply his information to the Police or
    Military.

7. Every citizen will arrange for the early or prior
    transfer to relatives or friends in safe areas
    of infirm members of his family, or of young
    children.

8. Every citizen who owns a motor vehicle will keep
    it full of petrol ready for emergency - by either
    economising in his ordinary use of petrol, or by
    conversion to producer gas[5] and charcoal.

9. Every citizen will have half-packed and ready
    for any emergency:
        A week's provisions per person, of small
    compass, as follows, or similar:
            ¼ lb. tea; ½ lb. sugar; 1 lb. slab chocolate;
            3x8 oz. tins beef; 2 lbs. rice; 1 large

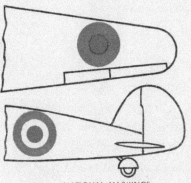

NATIONAL MARKINGS

British Aircraft

Note - The two markings shown are used in various
combinations and may sometimes be surrounded
by a yellow ring.

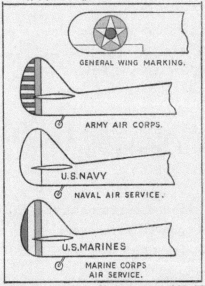

GENERAL WING MARKING.

ARMY AIR CORPS.

U.S.NAVY

NAVAL AIR SERVICE.

U.S.MARINES

MARINE CORPS
AIR SERVICE.

NATIONAL MARKING, AMERICAN AIRCRAFT.

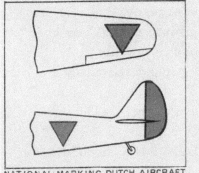

NATIONAL MARKING, DUTCH AIRCRAFT.

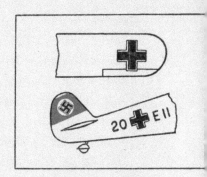

NATIONAL MARKING

GERMAN AIRCRAFT

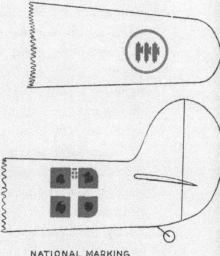

NATIONAL MARKING
ITALIAN AIRCRAFT.

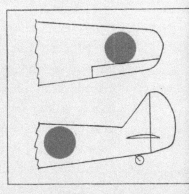

. NATIONAL MARKING .
. JAPANESE AIRCRAFT .

Bovril; petrol lighter and small supply
petrol, or 3 boxes matches; and
1 pkt. A.P.C. Powders[6]; small bottle iodine;
small roll ¾" adhesive plaster; 1×2" bandage;
and
1 heavy blanket or rug; 1 small plate;
knife, fork and spoon, mug, 1 qt. billycan;
tin opener with corkscrew; brush, comb and
small mirror; shaving gear; tooth brush and
paste; small cake soap; face washer or towel
(small); spare socks or stockings; sweater;
light waterproof cape or coat; home made
water bottle (e.g. 1 qt. flaggon, flannel
covered, to sling over shoulder).

(Women to wear strong low-heeled shoes and bush
attire.)

- and provide himself with a haversack and/or
swag.

10. Every citizen will make two identification discs
    for himself or herself out of plywood, leather,
    linen or other household material, mark on it in
    marking ink, or engraving, his or her Full Name,
    Occupation, Religion, Age and Address.
    - And wear it - one on wrist, one around neck.

11. Every citizen will plan emergency retreat for
    his women and children; the available motor cars
    will be reserved for such - able-bodied men over
    14 will have to retire on foot with swags.

12. Every citizen will pool his other vehicles
    (trucks, bicycles, carts, tractors), his tools,
    his essential goods, for collective use in
    retirement; and will hide or cache what he cannot
    pool or carry.

13. Every citizen will arrange for the emergency
    destruction of such of his goods as cannot be
    hidden or removed; and will see to it that he

leaves nothing moveable of use to the enemy,
other than house and furniture.

14. Every citizen will arrange to turn on the tap of
his water tanks before leaving, and puncture the
tank - and spoil his well as far as possible.

15. Every citizen will participate in civil
collaboration in either (i) The Volunteer
Defence Corps; (ii) The Naval Auxiliary Patrol;
(iii) A Guerilla Group; (iv) The N.E.S.-Air
Raid Precautions; (v) Labor Corps &c.; or make
camouflage nets, do First Aid, make bandages and
splints or guerilla uniforms, or make sandbags,
or dig trenches, or do camouflage work.
And work or drill after hours, and at weekends
and on holidays.

16. Every citizen will get busy at once - that is his
first battle station and war duty.

17. And every citizen, having arranged these things
will get his swag and tools, waterbag or water
bottle, billy, identity disc and ration card
ready to march in emergency with his mates in a
Civil Collaboration Column.

Battle Orders for the Plain Citizen - (ii) In
Business:

(i)   Every stock and cattle owner -
         (a) Will transfer his valuable stud stock
              to safe places outside possible danger
              zones in anticipation of emergency.
         (b) Will plan his route of retreat for
              whatever of his stock and cattle can
              be transferred in emergency, either to
              secluded bush paddocks, or inland via
              prescribed travelling stock routes and
              watering places.
         (c) Will plan to divert cattle to the military
              for use in exploding enemy mines &c.

(d) Will plan emergency destruction and/
     or slaughtering of beasts remaining
     in paddocks readily accessible to the
     infiltrating enemy - and the diversion
     through butchers or directly of meat to
     retiring military or civil forces.

(e) Will plan to have his plough horses, and
     harness complete with traces or chains,
     ready in emergency to transfer to the
     retiring military or civil forces; also
     his saddle horses and saddles (no saddle
     horses must fall into enemy hands).

(f) Will select quiet cattle for use as led
     pack animals.

(g) Before leaving destroy huts etc.,
     haystacks, all food and stores, dams,
     tanks and water supplies, wells,
     windmills, and homesteads which would
     serve as headquarters for the enemy.

(ii) Every butcher:

(a) Will keep in mild brine, the equivalent
     of one or two weeks' sales of meat.

(b) Will plan to use his delivery carts for
     mobile supply in retreat, getting his
     meat from cattle to be destroyed.

(iii) Every baker -

(a) Will plan for flour and yeast supply
     in retreat and for bushoven baking and
     delivery to the military and civil
     forces - using his civil delivery
     equipment.

(iv) Every Wholesaler and Retailer: -

(a) Will consign surplus stores and luxury
     goods to inland places of safety, or to
     safe caches.

(b) Will reduce his purchases to essentials
     equal to a month's turnover.

(c) Will sort out and rearrange his
     remaining stocks in two sections ready
     for emergency action:

   (i)   Essentials - to be removed in
          retreat, up to the capacity of
          his ordinary cartage equipment,
          including string, twine and bags.

   (ii)   Stores which can be given away to
          the needy in emergency.

   (iii) Stores which must be destroyed in
          emergency rather than that they
          should fall to enemy use.

(v)   <u>Every druggist, optician, watchmaker</u> -

(a) Will plan for safe removal or transfer to
     Medical Services, of (1) disinfectants,
     iodine, melasol[7] and the like;
     drugs, babies' foods, adhesive tape,
     gauze, lint, bandages, cotton wool,
     anaesthetics (ether, cocaine, morphia),
     surgical scissors, instruments &c.,
     hypodermic syringes, hot water bags,
     sedatives, aperients &c., soaps &c.
     (2) Optical lenses.
     (3) Watches.

(vi) <u>Every publican, wine and spirit vendor</u> -

(a) Will plan his stocks in the knowledge
     that in emergency, he will be required
     to destroy all beer, light wines and
     aerated drinks; and load all spirits and
     fortified wines on his civil-delivery
     vehicles for transfer to the Medical
     Services, Civil Casualty Clearing
     Stations and hospitals behind the
     fighting front.

> (b) Will arrange for his cooks and waitresses, with all available food supplies, knives, forks, spoons &c., to join up with Civilian Collaboration Column Commissariat.

(vii) <u>Every leather merchant and bootmaker</u> -
> (a) Will be required to have his stocks ready for transfer for the use of the civil or military forces in emergency.

(viii) <u>Every grocer, tobacconist, mercer and stationer</u> -
> (a) Will have ready to load and transfer emergency:
>> (i) Soaps, tobacco, mugs, panikins, knives and forks, matches, flints, tinned and dried foods, tea and sugar, salt, flour &c.
>> (ii) Dungarees; thick sox, shirts, oilskins, ground sheets, tennis nets (camouflage), dilly bags, onion bags.
>> (iii) Writing paper, pencils, pen and ink and envelopes - for messages.

(ix) <u>Every fisherman and boat owner</u> -
> (b) Will be ready to remove, hide, or sink all small boats that the enemy might requisition for extension of landings coastwise; and put engines out of action.
> (c) Recover and remove for camouflaging, all fishing nets.

(x) <u>Every farmer</u> -
> (a) Will plan to destroy haystacks and all other feed.
> (b) Will plan to harness horses to all available wheeled vehicles, load them with essential foods, and transport them

               to Civil Collaboration Column camps,
               along the route of retirement.

      (c) Supply all possible milk to the military
            or Civil Collaboration Column.

(xi)   Every blacksmith and plumber, tinsmith &c.

      (a) Will plan to bury his forge out of reach
            of the enemy or destroy it.

      (b) Will plan to make hand grenade
            containers.

(xii) Every garage and bowser proprietor -

      (a) Will plan to make available to the
            military medical services, or Civil
            Collaboration Column, the motor
            vehicles in his garages, spare parts,
            mechanical equipment &c.

      (b) Will see in emergency that none are
            left to the enemy, and if any have to
            be abandoned that the cylinder heads of
            motor vehicles are smashed and the rest
            destroyed.

      (c) Will remain in emergency to fill all
            military and civil transport with petrol
            and oil &c., and before retirement,
            subject to military requirement will
            empty his tanks, make the petrol useless
            with sugar, linseed oil, or by other
            means, or burn them.

      (d) Render themselves mobile and
            undertake repairs and services both
            for the fighting forces and the Civil
            Collaboration Column.

(xiii) Every Municipal or Shire Council, and water
       carrier -

      (a) Will keep all available water carts
            filled for emergency.

      (b) Will plan to make them available

for firefighting, military or Civil
Collaboration Column supply.

(c) Will retire with them in emergency,
refilling at towns, wells, waterholes
&c., replenishing horse-drawn water
carts serving the retiring civil forces.
(The horse drawn water carts should have
small taps plugged into the cross-pipe
at the rear, so that many water bottles
can be filled simultaneously - the carts
must be in charge of reliable persons
who will distribute water to necessitous
cases and allow only the minimum issue
for drinking purposes)

(xiv)   Every tractor owner -

(a) Will plan to drive his tractor in any
retirement.

(xv)   Every restaurant, cafe, teashop, ham & beef
shop proprietor -

(a) Will pool resources of food, kitchen
and service to establish a Civil
Collaboration Column canteen service,
render it mobile, and continue service
in retreat.

(xvi)   Every doctor, dentist, optician, X-ray
operator -

(a) Will join the Civil Collaboration Column
Medical Services.

(b) And stick to his job in retirement.

(xvii) Every railwayman -

(a) Will stick to his job to the last.

(b) Will organise for railway demolition to
military requirement.

(c) Will provide First Aid.

(xviii) Every policeman -

(a) Knows his jobs.

         (b) Plus dealing with looters, traitors, spies, enemy aliens &c.&c.

(xix) Every schoolteacher -

         (a) Will co-operate with Parents & Citizens' Association to organise the evacuation of children.

         (b) Will take care of children other than those in parents care.

(xx) Every Boy Scout -

         (a) Will learn to identify aeroplanes, particularly Japanese.

         (b) Will learn to take cover, move under cover, estimate distances, and report all information to the police.

         (c) Will practice throwing empty hand grenades.

         (d) Will commandeer all unused or unclaimed bicycles.

(xxi) Every postmaster and postal official -

         (a) Will stick to his job to the last.

         (b) Demolish.

         (c) Retire.

(xxii) Every sawmiller -

         (a) Will accelerate his production and consignment of timber.

         (b) Plan to retire on sawmills to the rear to provide another shift and to amalgamate, taking such essential parts and plant as he can transport.

         (c) Report to the Forest Officer.

(xxiii) Every butter and cheese factory manager -

         (a) Will plan amalgamations with other factories further back.

         (b) Will demolish the factory closed.

         (c) Report to the Agricultural Officer.

(xxiv)   <u>Every flourmill manager</u> -
     (a)   Will plan to keep his stocks low.
     (b)   Will plan to remove remaining stocks to the rear.

(xxv)   <u>Every timber-getter and charcoal burner</u> —
     (a)   Will stick to his job.
     (b)   Whilst moving back on other jobs.
     (c)   Will place himself under the direction of the Forest Officer for defence timber supply, firefighting &c.
     (d)   Will join the Forestry C.C.C.

(xxvi)   <u>Every carrier pigeon owner</u> -
     (a)   Will place his knowledge and his birds at the disposal of the military or the C.C.C. for use in war.

(xxvii)   <u>Every painter, carpenter, builder, artist</u> —
     (a)   Will engage in camouflaging.

(xxviii)   <u>Every unemployed or detached citizen</u> -
     (a)   Will report to the National Service Office for duty in the Labor Corps or any C.C.C.
     (b)   Or in emergency will attach himself to any C.C.C. needing help - pending organisation at the base C.C.C. Camp.

(xxix)   <u>Every citizen concerned will plan that</u> -
     (a)   All survey instruments are removed to the rear for the use of military and C.C.C.
     (b)   No map, even an ordinary tourist or advertising map is left to the enemy.
     (c)   Radios are destroyed.
     (d)   Cylinder heads of irremovable motor vehicles are destroyed.
     (e)   No wheel is left for enemy use.
     (f)   All axes, mattocks, shovels, picks, and other tools are removed for use behind

the lines - or securely hidden from the
enemy.

(g) No food is left to the enemy.

(h) No water remains in tanks.

(i) All garage equipment is removed or
destroyed.

(j) All tennis nets, string and twine are
commandeered for camouflage.

(k) All camp ovens are taken to the rear for
C.C.C. camp and canteen use.

(l) All soap is commandeered and removed.

Battle Orders for the Plain Citizen - (iii) As Amateur Combatants, Guerillas &c.

"Civilians are combatants", said the Prime
Minister on Anniversary Day.[8]

Since they are the people who are carrying on the
Battle of Production, they can join the Fighting
Forces only part-time - as Amateur Combatants!

Nor are there arms for all.

But they can physically resent the presence of
Japanese soldiers and gendarmerie in their streets
and homes -

We can do no less than the Spaniards did[9] -

And that was much!

We can go on strike - but that is not enough!

This is TOTAL war! There is little or no
distinction between the civilian and the soldier -
except that the former is unarmed, and must
collaborate with improvisations -

Australians can improvise.

Let us defend our homes and civilian rights with
home made weapons; in home made uniforms.

Or no uniforms at all (50% of the Japanese
soldiers in Malaya wore no uniform).

TOTAL WAR—AND TOTAL CITIZEN COLLABORATION   37

Meantime let us practice and exercise in our
homes, streets and parks.

1. Every citizen, <u>after hours</u>, will train in:

	(i)	A Volunteer Defence Corps.
or	(ii)	A Naval Auxiliary Patrol.
or	(iii)	An A.R.P.-N.E.S. organization.
or	(iv)	A Guerilla or Scouting Group.
or	(v)	A Boy Scouts or Girl Guide organisation.
or	(vi)	A Bushfire Brigade.
or	(vii)	An Ambulance or First Aid Group.
or	(viii)	
or	(ix)	

or practice individually or with his neighbours.

And learn how –

(a) To take cover.

(b) To move with as much use as possible of
cover; or in the dark of night; to scout.

(c) To dig in lying down.

(d) To estimate distances - lying down - (of
men at short and long distances, on levels
and gradients, of buildings, of street
widths, and so on).

(e) To make grenades; and to throw them so as
to score bullseyes every time.

(f) To "trip" a tank with a crowbar from the
doorways as it passes.

(g) To use weapons, particularly bayonets or
pikes.

(h) To out-trick the enemy's tricks.

These are the elements of guerilla warfare
taken from Wintringham's Penguin book - "New
Ways of War"[10] which is available to every Plain
Citizen!

Street and forest fighting against infiltration
parties and parachutists would be a feature of
invasion operations. And the Australian has this

initial advantage - he knows his streets; and he
knows his bush and its water supplies.

And he has his Australian fighting qualities
and initiative.

Volunteer bushmen who can make Molotov
cocktails or hand grenades, cast them with
accuracy, take cover and camouflage themselves
on roadsides, and make a get-away through what
may be burning forest.

- Constitute a measurably important anti-tank
group.

Note: When a tank is closed down, <u>it can't see above
it</u>, or along the ground within 15 or so feet;
or belly and <u>straddle</u> an obstacle 2'3"-2'6"
high.
Tank traps can be made of wide ditches filled
with logs and debris ready to light - or as
a deep belt of hardwood stumps 5'-6' apart,
2'3"-2'6" high, so that the tank can't
straddle and must foul its belly -
- or as slanting pole-lined ditches on banked
roadside to skid tanks over a declivity.
- or as banks of mill logs.
A wire stretched at 3 feet from the ground can
break an enemy cyclist's neck - or if slanted
obliquely at the right angle may sheer him
over a roadside declivity.
Boards with upturned nails will puncture tyres.
And so on.
Australians can improvise.

Roadside trees can be scarfed and sawn partly
through to be felled at the military moment to block
roads against enemy wheeled vehicles. Barking would
make them slippery, so that even tanks might be
momentarily delayed.

Abatis tank traps using felled hardwood trees can be arranged. (Mines would be harder to find amid a tangle of logs and debris than dug into plain earth) - and no doubt the military could add tear gas traps. A dose of stinging tree might sometimes be added to the enemy's discomfort.

Boulder and logs rolled from a hillside can contribute - and there is barbed wire for use from our fences - and dingo traps from the farms.

The Australian is a good axeman and has good axes - they may serve much the same purposes as the bayonet or the Ghurka kubri or the Chinese broadsword at close quarters.

And an ironbark pike might do as much damage as a bayonet.

In the event of invasion, first operations will likely take place largely in the forests - the Japanese infiltrated from every point through the jungles of Malaya in continuous outflanking moves.

If in summer-time, the bush will go ablaze.

Progress will be via water supplies and these must be commanded or destroyed. The enemy must be left without water as far as possible.

Bushranger guerillas can deal with infiltrating enemy requisitioning parties and scouts; succor and remove our wounded; guide, scout, and render supply to our soldiers, separated from their main forces; hunt out tank harbors at night; salvage abandoned stores at night in enemy-occupied areas; sabotage enemy supplies and wreck railway lines.

They can help themselves to enemy weapons and do some bush camouflaging, set up dummy guns, pill boxes and booby traps.

They may sometimes have to live very hard, and sometimes sustain themselves aboriginally.

The Australian bush offers very slender fare but here are its emergency rations:

Rabbits, birds and native game; scarce enough -
but can be shot or snared.

Fish and eels in most of the waterholes - (keep
fishing lines and hooks in the camp kit).

Roasted Alsophila pulp from the top of the tree
fern.

Roasted Bush Asparagus - the young shoots of the
Bulrush (Typha) in the water holes.

Boiled Kurrajong roots.

Kurrajong coffee from the roasted seeds.

(Note that explorer Leichhardt and his party
lived for some time on roast and boiled flying fox.)

ø/ CIVIL COLLABORATION COLUMNS AND THEIR
MOBILISATION:

Every citizen, having carried out his and her unit
battle orders as a private person and as a worker in
the peace-time economy, will report to his or her
Civil Collaboration Column.

In each Riding in each Shire, or in each separate
community, every male citizen over the age of 14, and
every female citizen employed in wartime duties, will
enrol in the Civil Collaboration Column and section
thereof corresponding to his or her place in the civil
sphere - vide the ten National Emergency Services.

These are -

1. Civil Administration C.C.C. - Police,
    justice, law: Child supervision (teaching),
    Banking and Finance, Council Services, Town
    Fire Brigades, A.R.P.-N.E.S.
2. Medical C.C.C. - hospitals, ambulances,
    doctors, dentists, opticians, druggists,
    X-ray operators, burial services, surgical
    supplies, Red Cross, First Aid &c.
3. Transport C.C.C. - Shipping, air, railways,
    tramways, road transport, garages and oil
    depots &c.

4. <u>Communication C.C.C.</u> - Post and telegraph,
   wireless, radio, newspapers, messenger,
   carrier pigeon.
5. <u>Commissariat C.C.C.</u> - Canteens, hotels,
   restaurants, bakers, butchers, grocers,
   cooks, waitresses &c.
6. <u>Primary Production C.C.C.</u> - Cattle, wheat,
   fish, sugar, tobacco, dairying, butter and
   cheese factories &c.
7. <u>Forestry C.C.C.</u> - Timber supply, forest
   officers, timber-getters, sawmills,
   woodworkers, charcoal burners, bushfire
   brigades &c.
8. <u>Miners C.C.C.</u> - Coal, minerals &c.
9. <u>Leather, rubber and textiles C.C.C.</u> -
   Operators therein.
10. <u>Mechanical C.C.C.</u> - Mechanics, fitters,
    plumbers, tinsmiths &c.
11. <u>Building and Camouflage C.C.C.</u> - Architects,
    carpenters, painters &c.
12. <u>Labor and demolition C.C.C.</u> - Unattached
    labor.

In each Shire, or in each separate community, a
meeting will be called for each C.C.C. for enrolment,
and for the election of officers and chairman.

Every citizen will report in writing to the
Secretary on the fulfilment of his Citizen Battle
orders, and the Secretary will compile and summarise
the whole in a report for consideration of a second
meeting immediately following, to prepare a C.C.C.
draft plan for submission to —

ø/ A COMMITTEE OF CIVIL COLLABORATION COLUMNS (C.C.C.C.):

This Committee will consist of the elected
chairmen of the twelve Columns or their

representatives, with Secretary and clerical staff
to be provided by the State Government.

- And will become the district consultative
committee to -

- A DISTRICT C.C.C. COMMISSIONER -

to be appointed by the State Government.

It will prepare from the C.C.C. draft plans a
composite C.C.C.C. draft plan - and the District
C.C.C. Commissioner therefrom will draft the
complete district plan in detail to conform to
the Master Plan, and submit it for the approval of
Government.

Thereupon the District Plan will become law
and will be administered by the District C.C.C.
Commissioner and policed by the Police, reinforced
by special police.

Until this be done, the District C.C.C.
Commissioner may adopt and implement in emergency a
provisional draft plan.

ø/ THE THEME OF THE C.C.C. PLAN:

The theme of the C.C.C. plans will be, that:

ø/ No air raid, no shellings, no civil casualties
   therefrom, and no rumor or gossip will intimidate
   the working population to cessation of work,
   evacuation, or stampede; But will stimulate it
   to work harder and engage part-time in emergency
   auxiliaries to counter the enemy action.

ø/ Organising meantime for the coastal danger
   zones - whilst there is time -

   (i)   The entire suspension of peace-time
          development.

   (ii)   The implementation and extension of peace-
          time decentralisation principles.

   (iii) The reduction of war-time non-essential
          industries, and the extension of war-time
          essential industries and services.

(iv)   The rationalisation of remaining
       industry; the amalgamation of sawmills,
       butter, cheese and other factories, and
       their transport.

(v)   The transfer inland or otherwise of
       displaced factories, of spare machinery
       and parts, of timber stocks, of stud
       stock, of luxury goods.

(vi)   The voluntary evacuation of the infirm,
       of children under 16, and of mothers and
       women over 16 not voluntarily attached
       to C.C.C.

ø/ And having ready, for automatic-instant unit and
   group implementation at the invasion signal for
   any sector, a plan for:

(i)   Evacuation by (a) evacuation trains; and
       (b) private motor cars with their last
       fill of petrol, the remaining infirm,
       children and unrequired women.

(ii)   Civil mobilisation and withdrawal, by
       personal and group action, of the working
       population and of all available supplies
       of cattle &c., to pre-selected C.C.C.
       assembly points behind the fighting front
       for reorganisation to mobile functioning.

(iii) Salvage and demolition, search party and
       rescue work.

ø/ And having located beforehand -
   Caches and hiding places for stores. Watering
   place and C.C.C. assembly points and camps in the
   forests. Bush roads and tracks, and travelling
   stock routes. Forest Stations.

Each C.C.C. will draft its own plan and submit to
the District Commissioner for co-ordination with the
District Plan, in consultation with the C.C.C.C. and

for issue back to each C.C.C. when finally fitted to the District Plan and approved for implementation.

In any emergency pending this, each C.C.C. will operate its plan as co-operatively as possible with its fellow Citizen Collaboration Columns.

Employers and employees and their civil organisation will automatically become part of the C.C.C. war organisation and will continue to function in their civil employment as part of this C.C.C. organisation as fully as war circumstances will permit, but in accordance with the C.C.C. action detail.

Each C.C.C. will operate the transport available to it from its own civil economy; this transport will remain in its original ownership unless and until it is impressed.

The concept is that the civil economy becomes mobile and organised to function in war under original ownership and employer-employee arrangements, but functioning to C.C.C. plan – unless and until it is absorbed into the military organisation of the country.

Men who find themselves unemployed or unattached to a C.C.C., will report for duty to the nearest National Service Officer, for enrolment in the Labor or other C.C.C. - or in emergency may report for duty to a functioning C.C.C., or to the nearest Forest Station or police station.

Any man over 16 not so enrolled will not be entitled to war rations and may be classed as a deserter.

Rates of pay for the Labor Corps or for men attached to C.C.Cs. not on employer pay rolls, will be equivalent to military rates.

Each man must be self-contained, carrying his swag, with a week's provisions, a water bag or water

bottle and a billy; and bringing his axe, mattock,
shovel, or other tools; he must wear his identity
discs and carry a war ration card.

Briefly, should any sector be imminently
threatened by enemy landing from sea or air, the men
will instantly see the women, children and infirm
off to places of safety by train or civil motor car,
and themselves take to the bush as C.C.Cs., with
all available material and remaining transport, and
there organise to mobile functioning, serving and
supporting the fighting forces as required by the
military authorities.

This has been done in China without plan, and in
Russia to pre-arranged plan.

Australians can do no less! Country people will
have little difficulty in accommodating themselves
to an arduous open-air living; many city dwellers
know how to hike and camp.

There is no snow in Australia!

The limiting factor is water!

The first tasks in the chain of C.C.C. invasion
duties are to locate the water supplies along the
primary and subsidiary lines of withdrawal, to
pre-select C.C.C. camps at these water supplies,
and to see that even from the most secluded camp
a line of retreat remains open even if only on foot
with swags.

The section on "Coastal Routes and Terrain"
indicates these broadly -

Bush sawmills, forest stations, sleepergetters
and cattle drovers' camps, dams, wells and water
holes give the local clues.

It will be necessary to pre-select the C.C.C.
camps - to estimate beforehand how many people
each could sustain and for what period, to rough
out camping and parking places and supply dumps
and caches, to camouflage them from the air, to

protect them from bush fires, to screen them from
infiltrating parties, to defend them by barricades
and trenches, and to plan retreat.

Calculating the number of male civilians to
be mobilised in the C.C.Cs., these can then be
apportioned by villages or communities to the pre-
selected camps.

Forest Stations can become C.C.C. headquarters -
their stores and tool depots and first aid
equipment, maps, telephone &c. at the service of
such. Fire lookouts, towers and crows nests can
become observation posts. Water filling posts and
water trucks can serve.

All timber workers (C.C.C. Forestry) should
regard the Forest Stations as their assembly
points, whence military timber requirements can
be dealt with, charcoal supplies arranged for
producer gas trucks, and guiding, scouting, counter
infiltration, and bushfire defence and offence
arranged.

There will have to be lines of bush communications
between the C.C.C. and inland and with the
military; and evacuation of wounded and unfit.
Severe rationing is inevitable and supply must be
developed at the expense of the enemy. There will
have to be supply raids and guerilla warfare - with
or without military weapons or uniforms. There will
be aeroplane machine gunning attacks, infiltrating
enemy parties, bushfires - or floods.

There will be many difficulties - but fewer than
those which would befall if civilians remained as
Japanese hostages.

Knowing the bush better than the invader the
C.C.Cs. will be able to render helpful service to
the fighting forces -
(1) By maintaining and supplying themselves as
    organised groups.

(2) By auxiliary service to the military according
    to their C.C.C.

(3) By providing military reinforcements as armies
    become available - preferably from the enemy!

(4) By constituting a flanking screen to guard
    against the out-flanking of our fighting men.

(5) By the defensive and offensive use of bush fires;
    the digging of trenches, the construction of
    tank traps, the near-felling of roadside trees
    ready to block roads, the improvisation of
    barbed wire entanglements.

(6) By the removal or reversal of sign posts and the
    stationing of traffic directors and guides.

(7) By the supply of timber and charcoal, the
    evacuation and slaughtering of cattle, and the
    organisation of meat supply, the provision and
    rationing of food at the C.C.C. camps.

ø/ INVASION ACTION:

The ringing of church and other bells or the
blowing of motor horns cease in the rural coastal
regions.

In the event of imminent enemy invasion by landing
from sea or air, the Invasion Action signal will be
the ringing of such bells and the blowing of such
horns.

Instantly thereupon -

1. EVERY CITIZEN WILL EVACUATE HIS REMAINING
   CHILDREN, INFIRM, AND WOMEN NOT VOLUNTARILY
   ENGAGED IN C.C.C. WAR DUTIES.

   (At Penang only half an hour was available!)
   Evacuation will be by special evacuation
   trains; or by pre-selected roads and routes
   inland; the citizen using the private motor car or
   conveyance which he has reserved for the purpose.

   (i)   Use only motor cars, utilities and horse
          driven vehicles; trucks and bullock and

THIS PROBLEM OF SENDING YOUR CHILD AWAY

Doctors discuss raid effects on youngsters of all ages

By MARGARET RICHARDS

"I don't know which would make me more unhappy —bombs or leaving mummy and daddy and living with people who don't really love me."

This is what a little girl of ten years told me when I asked her if she was going to be evacuated to the country.

THE psychological turmoil of this small child is only one of the problems of evacuation. Parents are trying to make up their minds just what to do.

Difficult pros. and cons. of the domestic side have to be weighed.

There is the desire of the wife to share with her husband whatever danger may come, the financial burden of supporting two households, and the uprooting of children from schools where they have already found their feet.

But, actually, these problems are only minor in relation to determining the mental and physical well-being of the children.

Some interesting opinions on the evacuation of children have been expressed by doctors.

A well-known Sydney medical man, in planning the evacuation of children, stated that all children under 12 should be evacuated, and at once. At the Government's expense, if necessary.

He considers that the average child, older than 12, has passed the totally impressionable age.

An English doctor, Dr. W. E. R. Mons, a trained psychologist, is heartily in favor of the evacuation of children, no matter what their age.

He vigorously attacks the conduct of thousands of parents who have taken their children back from evacuation districts to their own homes in target areas.

"If there's another raid, the children can be evacuated again," is the dangerous outlook of the parents which he condemns.

But the effect of that one "extra" raid may do untold harm to the child.

It is impossible to tell immediately what reaction will result. Very possibly, the child himself will not know.

In one case cited by Dr. Mons, a boy had, according to his own statement, slept through a raid, but the realisation next day of how near death he had been caused a severe shock, none the less serious because it was delayed.

Like adults, children "crack hardly," and their casual air at assumed normality may be far removed from the real psychological reaction.

Besides, that one "extra" raid may undo in a few moments all the curative value of months in districts out of the line of fire.

Difficult children

WE heard much at the beginning of the war regarding "difficult evacuation children" in England, and no doubt many of us have wondered if families offering accommodation in Australia to city children would be faced with the same problems.

But these difficulties were not necessarily the children's fault. Some of them, of course, would be "difficult" even in their normal life and normal environment. In their own homes they would be looked at, as "unmanageables."

But the majority of the "difficult evacuation children" were "difficult" only because of their subjection to bombing—or, almost equally important—because of their fear of bombing.

It was found that formerly good and intelligent children became suddenly obstreperous, destructive, mischievous, lazy, played truant from school and, in short, unmanageable in the billet to which they had been evacuated.

In some cases the teacher of the new school expressed doubt about the pupil's mental normality, where the previous report had stated him to be up to "scholarship standard."

The children also showed marked inability to know what to do with themselves.

They tired of one thing after another in rapid succession—legitimate amusement and mischief both proving equally lacking in attraction after a few minutes.

The children became a nuisance to themselves as well as to others.

They seemed to possess deep resentment against the adults who had failed to provide that security and protection which is every child's birthright; the collapse of all the values which education had carefully built up so far;

Death became a personal problem, and parental authority was no longer a safe shield against the direct threat of extinction.

Such problems are affecting British children who were previously normal—healthy, intelligent, well-behaved—and they are problems which will affect Australian children unless they are removed in time from our danger zones.

The strain of parting with parents to take up a new life with possibly critical strangers is difficult for children.

Those who have offered their homes and those who will be helping with evacuated children will have to remember that, whether subjected to air raids or not, the children will need infinite sympathy and understanding.

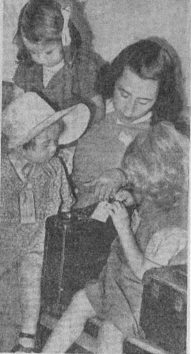

ENGLISH MOTHERS sadly say farewell to their children en route to areas safe from bombing.

EVACUATION rehearsals are in full swing at Sydney day-nurseries. Miss C. Hamilton, one of the voluntary workers at the Woolloomooloo nursery, with three of the 600 children who will be evacuated in the event of emergency.

horse teams must be reserved from this
use for the express purpose of removal of
essential stores and for the supply and
service of the fighting forces.

(ii)   No car or vehicle must travel the route of
civil retirement unless the entire seating
accommodation is filled with children,
infirm, or women. (Men may drive only if
women drivers are not available).

(iii) Each person must carry a week's provisions
of small compass; personal documents and
valuables may be taken but no goods or
chattels; a self-provided identity disc
must be worn. (No luxury goods may be
taken - these must be cached or destroyed).

(iv)   Travel must be by defined non-military
routes, via defined camping places to
defined destinations by families and Shire
communities.

(v)   Police may detail extra cars or trucks to
accommodate children, infirm or women not
catered for by the above arrangements; the
assembly point will be the nearest police
station.

(vi)   At their destination, evacuees will
engage in making camouflage nets, C.C.C.
uniforms, bandages, and will arrange with
the reception authorities for future
supply of stores for their menfolk in
the C.C.Cs., and for the maintenance of
communications.

2. EVERY CITIZEN WILL CARRY OUT HIS UNIT ACTION AS
MEMBER OF A C.C.C.: AND EVERY C.C.C. AS SUCH WILL
IMPLEMENT ITS INVASION ACTION CODE.

Firstly, each C.C.C. within its civil sphere,
and by its citizen units, and with the transport

available to it and them from that sphere, will
instantly:
(a) Load its trucks and vehicles to capacity with
   essential stores, e.g.
   (i)   Food and groceries, flour from flour
          mills, tea and sugar, soap, matches,
          tobacco, tinned and dried foods.
   (i(a) Spirits and fortified wines.
   (ii)   Petrol and oils (including castor oil
          for lubrication).
   (iii) Tools and essential machinery parts.
   (iv)   Boots and shoes and leather.
   (v)   All articles required for medical
          attention, i.e. bandages,
          disinfectants, iodine, melasol and the
          like; drugs, babies' food, adhesive
          tape, gauze, lint, cotton wool,
          anaesthetics (ether, cocaine etc.),
          surgical scissors, instruments etc.,
          hypodermic syringes, morphia &c.; hot
          water bags, aperients, sedatives &c.
   (vi)   Optical lenses, survey instruments,
          watches, flints, writing paper, ink,
          pens, pencils and envelopes.
   (vii) A small parcel of clothing essentials,
          dungarees, shirts, thick sox, oilskins,
          ground sheets.
   (viii) Camp ovens (although white ant mounds
          can be converted into bush camp ovens).
   (ix)   Fishing and tennis nets, and so on -
          vide C.C.C. action plans.
   (x)   Bicycles.
 - and remove these to the first C.C.C. camp
behind the fighting front and deliver to the
Camp Q.M.
   (Usually the storekeeper-owner, playing his
part in his C.C.C. will carry out this removal

himself, with assistance, and may be assigned by
the Camp Q.M. to distribute at the camp to C.C.C.
members per rationed card and under Government
guarantee; or to transfer them to second or
further C.C.C. camps.

If there be time, a second trip may be made –
otherwise irremovable essential supplies to
be cached beyond discovery by the enemy or
destroyed by destruction parties).

And thereafter each C.C.C. will proceed
urgently as per its Action Plan.

3. All available water carts, including Council
watering carts, must be filled and removed also
along the line of retreat; and except for water
supplies required for firefighting or designated
by the fighting forces for their use, all water
tank taps must be turned on, and all other water
supplies destroyed beyond the needs of a thirsty
enemy.

Water trucks (Council and private ones
used for firefighting) will fill up at water
supplies (towns, wells, waterholes &c.) off the
evacuation routes and will replenish horse drawn
water carts that will accompany the evacuees.
The horse drawn water carts should have small
taps plugged into the cross pipe at rear so that
many water bottles may be filled simultaneously;
the carts must be in charge of reliable persons
who will distribute water to necessitous cases
and not allow any except the minimum for drinking
purposes to be issued.

4. Route cards will be issued by the police when
the C.C.C. vehicle is loaded; these will
show destination and will act as a pass along
route and will allow driver to obtain petrol
or charcoal. N.R.M.A. and R.A.C.A. will be

stationed at road turn-offs along lines of route
to examine and issue route cards, direct traffic
regarding routes to be followed (i.e. if roads
are in military use, bridges destroyed &c.),
supervise fuel replenishment &c.

(Japanese airplanes will try to machine gun
the evacuating cars - therefore have them ready
camouflaged, follow the bush roads, and keep to
the edge under cover.

5. Rearguard salvaging and search parties will
   recover whatever can be removed of what is left,
   round up stragglers, aliens, spies, traitors;
   whilst the Medical Services C.C.C. rescues the
   wounded.

6. Destruction of irremovable essential goods will
   proceed simultaneously by unit citizen action,
   supplemented by C.C.C. action:
   e.g. beer, light wines and spirits; small
   boats not designated for military use; radios;
   irremovable vehicles; wheels; axes, mattocks,
   tools, garage equipment, food, clothing;
   haystacks and horse feed; cattle, stock and pigs;
   - and anything else of which the enemy may make
   use against us.

ø/ DUTIES OF THE C.C.Cs.:

   The sketches hereunder need complete elaboration
and timing, and are intended only to give a first
impression of the duties of some of the C.C.Cs.

1. FORESTRY (including Bush Fire Brigades):
   The District Forester will be the Actions
   Officer:
   (i)   Fire control:
          — to detect and extinguish enemy
            bushfires.
          — to make and control offensive fires on
            military orders

- to maintain lookouts, patrols and
  scouting, and to supply guides.
- to prepare C.C.C. camp fireplaces and
  protect C.C.C. camps from loose fires.

(ii)   Sawmilling:
- to supervise the operation, or transfer
  of bush sawmills, and the supply of sawn
  timber.

(iii) Charcoal:
- to supervise the manufacture and supply
  of charcoal.

(iv)   Timber cutting:
- to provide hewn, split, and pole
  material for defence requirements.
- to organise and control logging
  operations and haulage.
- to form special mobile parties of storm
  cutters to supply the fighting front
  with timber requirements at urgent call
  within danger areas. These parties will
  be formed on military lines, be self-
  contained and possess such mobility
  that they can be quickly transferred
  from district to district by their own
  transport.

(v)   Roading and tank traps:
- using forestry plant and equipment.
- to make roads for timber supply.
- clear bush roads for military use.
- prepare tank traps and fill them with
  logs and debris for burning, or as
  conventional traps.

2. LABOR (Defence Constructions):

An engineer of the Main Roads Board, Public
Works Department or Shire, will be the Actions
Officer:

To dig trenches and tank traps at military
  requirement.
To cache or destroy stores.
To build and repair bridges.
To co-operate with bushfire fighting forces.
Obtain and set barbed wire defence.
Loading and unloading at dumps and rail sidings
  &c.
Remove explosives.
Build and repair roads.
Erect camouflage.
Any other normal work as called upon by
  military.

3. ENGINEERS:

All N.R.M.A. and R.A.C.A. men, garage owners
and mechanics from garages and other factories,
with such transport as is essential to their
mobility, will:

(i)   Supply petrol, oil, parts;
(ii)   Remove, hide or destroy all mechanical
       equipment, oils and stores.
(iii) Render themselves mobile, and undertake
       repairs &c. for both the military and the
       Commandos along the military rear.

4. COMMISSARIAT:

This Column will be composed of the butchers,
bakers, grocers, druggists, fruiterers, cafes,
cooks, and other civil community purveyors and
foodstuffs and the like; also bootmakers - with
the transport used by them in their civil economy.

This transport will be loaded to capacity
and will report to the Camp Q.M. at the nearest
C.C.C. camp.

The District Action Officer will be assisted
by the principal caterers.

Their function will be to provide canteen service for the Columns and the fighting forces.

War rationing will prevail, and cards must be kept.

5. PRIMARY PRODUCTION:

The District Agricultural Department Officer will assume command as District Action Officer.

Cattle and stock owners will select the best half of their herds and flocks, and will drive them via appointed stock routes and secluded camping spots along the line of retreat - milking en route if possible, for supply to C.C.C. camps, or slaughtering tired beasts for similar use.

Quiet cattle can be used as pack animals, if led only.

The second half of the herds and flocks will remain on the farms under men to be detailed by their owners - to be milked or slaughtered for the service of the fighting front.

Those which cannot be so used must be driven off into the bush - if about to be captured - or destroyed.

Water tank taps to be opened; other water supply if possible to be destroyed, if about to be captured. All water tank roof catchment and otherwise to be punctured.

Food supplies to be cached or destroyed, if about to be captured.

Probably butcher's sheep should be taken back first with most milkers and slaughter cattle and the balance of milkers and cattle left for supply to military, as the big stock can travel faster.

6. MEDICAL SERVICES:

The senior resident doctor will be the District Action Officer; a Deputy should also be appointed.

This C.C.C. will consist of evacuated doctors, dentists, hospital staffs, Ambulance, First Aid groups, funeral directors and the like.

Horse drawn First Aid carts will accompany evacuees; these will give first aid to those suffering minor injuries or collapse; they will be in charge of persons who will refuse to be imposed upon.

Motor ambulances will convey serious cases (too serious for first aid carts to handle) to next outward stopping place, where doctor (there will be one stationed at a casualty clearing station at each stopping place), will arrange for patient, if he considers necessary, to be taken to a base hospital.

Motor hearses should be converted into ambulances.

ADDENDA NOTES -

1. Coastal gaols should be evacuated inland.
2. Forestry Prison Camps at Mannus, Glen Innes and Oberon are now understaffed with prisoners, and the remainder could probably be concentrated at one of these, leaving two for the reception of (a) Aliens; (b) Reformatory boys.
3. Enemy prisoners-of-war and aliens could be probably used in inland areas for wood cutting and charcoal burning, logging, roadwork in the Rylestone mountain forests, water supply, or building reception accommodation.
4. Lubricating oil is more essential even than petrol; the seeds of the castor oil plant contain 50% of oil, and a screw press suffices to extract the oil.

The castor oil plant can be grown successfully inland in dry Climatic Zones 5.6 and 7.6. It has easy and rapid growth, copious seeding, and gives early return.

5. New Zealand flax produces a fibre which when
   properly dressed withstands moisture as well as
   the best manilla rope. It should flourish on the
   Blue Mountains.
6. Country plumbers and mechanics could turn out
   hand-grenade containers for guerilla use.
7. Secret aerodromes and emergency landing places
   could be located back from the coastal front,
   and probably be carried out of original bush to
   a defensive design.

   The evolution of aerodromes has been:

   (a)   Complete clearing and levelling in peace-
         time, and erection of one very prominent
         hangar.
   (b)   Defence in wartime by obstruction &c. -
         e.g. stumps on other than fairways &c. and
         by camouflage &c.

   This suggests that emergency wartime
   aerodromes can be the more quickly and logically
   devised by:

   (a)   Felling all trees to a stump height of
         3 feet.
   (b)   Grubbing and levelling only the fairways,
         viz. SE-NW, NE-SW, and N-S: and leaving
         the stumps on the unoccupied zones, and
         pointing them so that (a) parachutists
         landing on them will be injured; (b)
         tanks after breaking off the points will
         find their bellies fouled at 2'3"-2'6";
         (c) head and shoulder protection will be
         afforded to defenders. The resultant logs
         may also be left, arranged radially so as
         to assist in the fouling. A fire should be
         passed over the felling to burn all debris
         except the stumps and logs.
   (c)   Building several small hangars within the
         edge of natural cover.

A LAYMAN IDEA OF A
DEFENSIVE AERODROME
CARVED OUT OF ORIGINAL BUSH

A · Separated Hangars.
B · Stump area after burning off
C · Natural cover · Original
D · Runways.
E · Centre trap
F · Tarmac

Diagramatically, the layman imagines something like the attached (see diagram).

The design of a <u>defended</u> aerodrome could thus be carved out of the original standing timber to the finished shape! - more expeditiously and more economically than by peace-to-war conversion.

The fairways could be covered by gunfire or traps at the centre against enemy aeroplanes or parachutists - and carry a centre guide line as on highways, with sunken lights if necessary.

8. Cattle can be used to explode enemy mines and provide a screen for advancing troops.

9. Coastal sawmills should be worked as many shifts as possible, and sawn stocks transferred inland for reception accommodation, and reserve supplies.

10. Water supplies control route: in many areas these are not abundant; the major ones should be commanded; in a retreat the minor ones could sometimes be poisoned.

11. Aboriginal trackers and aborigines on occasion can be usefully employed in guerilla work.

12. The Japanese manifestos declare: "Those who do not obey, or who take hostile actions against the Japanese Forces will be shot. Co-operate with the Japanese forces."

No Australian will co-operate with the Japanese forces: therefore there is no alternative but to definitely organise the contrary!

13. Caches should be established beforehand in the bush - of grenades, tools, materials and supplies - for the use of the C.C.C. and guerillas.

DEFENCE OF SYDNEY (Newcastle-Pt. Kembla):

ø/ NO EVACUATION - EVEN FOR SCHOOL CHILDREN:

There can be no evacuation from this urban zone of concentrated industry,

- but only withdrawal sector by sector under stress of invasion.

Indeed such evacuation, voluntary or otherwise, as can be organised would be cancelled out by war concentrations and supply services, and by the arrival of evacuees from other countries.

We can only endeavor to reduce war-time congestions, and avert stampede and confusion by a plan of organised emergency withdrawal in which every citizen has his part prior-defined.

Every institution and organisation, private or Governmental, should re-orient its activities to the war emergency, and to state for approval the war functions which it can assume as an existing staff organisation. (This method will often give quicker and better controlled results with greater responsibility than by disintegration of existing organisations to establish new loose voluntary part-time organisations. The existing management can then be held responsible to the supreme Civil Collaboration Management for approved war functions.)

A decentralisation policy should operate urgently - and the first step would probably be the adjustment of railway freight rates and fares to stimulate this.

Munitions industries should be transferred or duplicated inland. (Slazenger's, making rifle stocks out of Coachwood, Frederick Rose & Co., making airplane ply out of Coachwood logs, could function closer to their sources of supply of raw material at Armidale.)

In sectors exposed to air raids and shellings –
but well defended and not imminent landings –
  Evacuation should not be a policy!
  This includes school children!
ø/ At 18 and over, children are men and women for
   the purpose of war.
ø/ Mothers and young children should not be
   separated: and wives prefer to remain with their
   husbands: their evacuation should be voluntary
   only: facilities for voluntary evacuation and
   dispersal through inland country towns should
   be developed – although even this may not hold
   against human nature.
ø/ Boys and girls of 14-18, however, are the
   soldiers of 1943/46, and the post-war
   generation – these should be withdrawn to
   country bases for war and post-war training.

1. PLANS SHOULD BE PREPARED FOR THE RETIREMENT OF
   THE CIVIL POPULATION FROM THE INDUSTRIAL URBAN
   AREAS ONLY IN THE EVENT OF NECESSITY DUE TO
   IMMINENT ENEMY LANDING OR ADVANCE, AND THEN ONLY
   FROM AFFECTED SECTORS.
   (The C.C.C. rural organisation could be
   developed for this purpose.)
2. BOYS AND GIRLS OF 14-18 SHOULD BE WITHDRAWN TO
   COUNTRY BASES FOR WAR AND POST-WAR TRAINING – AS
   CADETS.
     1. Each to be vocationally analysed, and posted
        to the training group indicated thereby.
     2. School training to be continued accordingly.
     3. With auxiliary training in war services.

ø/ EMERGENCY WATER SUPPLIES VITAL:
  The vital question, however, is: "Is Sydney to die
of thirst, or stampede inland?"

In Hongkong the Japanese bombed the water
supplies and pipes before they passed on to military
objectives.

Obviously that would happen here!

The water supply position should be put on a war
basis at once by:-

(a) Stimulation of voluntary well-sinking and dam-
    sinking instantly by home dwellers.

(b) Severest rationing of water supply for both
    homes and factories, in districts where water is
    available by shallow boring, e.g. Botany, North
    Shore Line.

(c) Rain tanks &c. to be installed as far as
    possible.

(d) Municipalities and Shires to be instructed to
    organise emergency water supply for their areas,
    and to be responsible for delivery to key points
    in emergency:

    (i)   Establishment of municipal wells and bores
           (see the Youhotsky Scheme [later in this
           chapter]).

    (ii)   Organising and extending their water cart
           services against emergency, improvising
           additions, and keeping them full.

    (iii) Selecting and converting sunken tennis
           courts, baths, and dam sites into local
           auxiliary reservoirs.

    (iv)   Preparing plans &c. for salt water
           distillations.

    (v)   Arranging deliveries in emergency.

    (vi)   Relaxing the normal peace-time water
           standards - domestic boiling to be
           prescribed where considered necessary.

    (vii) Use of salt water for street flushing and
           fire fighting.

(e) Water Board to lay small emergency pipe lines to selected key points against the possibility of destruction of main pipe lines.
(f) Water supply for non-essential industry to be (a) severely rationed; (b) cut off in emergency.
(g) In the outer suburbs, where the pan system will suffice, sewerage extension should cease, and existing sewerage disconnected, with reversion to the pan system.
(h) Householders to fill and keep filled in containers (bottles if nothing better) a week's supply of drinking water (only).
(i) Existing industrial bores to be deepened at once.
(j) Motor radiators even in unused cars to be kept filled.
(k) Railway Department to organise emergency water carriage to the city.

Provisional evacuation camps should be prepared just below the main reservoirs (but off the water course), so as not to contaminate the water supply and so as to be assured of water supply in the event of pipeline destruction. Then in the event of inadequate emergency supply in the city, these provisional evacuation camps can accommodate the surplus population from water famine areas, pending the organisation of evacuation inland.

ø/ RECEPTION ORGANISATION INLAND:

Every inland community should call a public meeting and organise and officer a Reception Organisation Committee:
— To make an inventory of available empty houses; stores, offices and meeting rooms.
— To ascertain capacity and potentiality of boarding houses, room letting, paying guests, billeting &c.

- To list, stating rents, all living accommodation which could be mobilised in emergency.
- To define, without progress committee propaganda, the authentic power and industrial possibilities of its location under a decentralisation policy - and to make a brief and guaranteed business statement of practical business propositions.
- To state briefly and precisely, the accommodation, drill ground, or aerodrome potentialities of its golf courses, clubs, race-courses and showgrounds.
- To define the water supply capacity of its location - and to demarcate emergency water supplies in its locality.
- To state its hospital capacity and extension potential.
- To plan for emergency absorption of (a) Youth trainees 14-18; (b) Voluntary evacuees; (c) Invasion evacuees.

"This'll be one bit of information the Japs won't get!"

R.300

> John A. Youhotsky,
> 9 George Street,
> Pennant Hills, N.S.W.,
> 27th January, 1942.

Dear Sir,

Emergency Water Supply for Sydney.

The weakest link in the defence of Sydney Metropolitan Area is undoubtedly its water supply. This water supply is dangerously inadequate due to drought, and extremely vulnerable, because it depends on distant dams and long pipelines.

The Japanese tactics in similar cases were always to attack and interrupt water supply rather than try to overcome the purely military centres of resistance. Such was the case in the earlier wars: Port Arthur in the Russo-Japanese war of 1905, and Tsingtao in the war of 1914. Hongkong fell much sooner than anticipated because the Japanese struck not only on the catchment dams, but on the pipelines of Victoria well before they attacked any military fortifications. Lack of water forced the surrender of the garrison.

One of the main difficulties of the defence of Singapore will again be the fact that sources of water are on the mainland, scores of miles from the perimeter of the fortress proper.

This is a most dangerous situation, and the case of Sydney is exactly similar!

As early as 1940 it appeared that emergency was unavoidable and I published in the December issue of 1940 "Australasian Engineer" an article pointing out the military weaknesses of Sydney water supply, as well as indicating some corrective measures.

I enclose a copy of this Journal, and call your attention to page 3 &c. in it.

UNDERGROUND SUPPLY FOR EMERGENCY:

My main thesis is that sufficient underground
supply could be had within the Sydney metropolitan
area, and should be immediately developed as an
emergency proposition. This is necessary because:-

(1) Dams on the catchment areas might fall into
    enemy hands before any attempt be made to
    attack the capital, which could be forced into
    submission through lack of water.
(2) Water of all open reservoirs can be poisoned
    (or bacterially infected) from enemy aircraft.
    Poisoning of the smaller reservoirs and wells by
    Germans in Russia is being reported now. All our
    water comes from open storage.
(3) A combination of the above two cases is quite
    feasible, namely, the distant dams might be
    seized, while water in the nearer ones might
    be poisoned (Woronora and Warragamba, and open
    channel from Prospect).

BOTANY:

Under the emergency circumstances, the water
riches of Botany should be instantly tapped and
widespread public and private sinking of bores or
dug-wells should be encouraged in all suburbs.

In accordance with Water Board's data, in the
sands of Botany, a few feet under the ground, is
a store of 31,000 million gallons of water. This
is 1½ times more than the sum total of all storage
reservoirs of the Water Board at present! With the
use of about 20 gals. per capita per day, water
stored at Botany would be sufficient for about
3 years. A siege of such a duration has never yet
been recorded in history.

20 gallons per day per capita is the normal
consumption of Leningrad, Moscow, and other Russian

cities where water is charged in proportion to
metered consumption, and should be quite adequate
for citizens of Sydney also.

PRACTICAL SCHEME:

   I propose to subdivide the whole area of Botany
of about 7,000 acres (containing as per Water Board
data about 31,000 million gallons in underground
storage in sands) into 60 sub-areas of 117 acres,
and sink a bore of 12" in each of these sub-areas.
The electrical (or power) turbine deep well pump
will yield about 25,000 gallons per hour from such
a 12" bore. With the population of Sydney taken
at 1,500,000, then 60 wells like this will be
sufficient:

$$\frac{1,500,000 \text{ men} \times 20 \text{ gals.}}{25,000 \text{ gals./hour} \times 20 \text{ working hours a day}} = 60 \text{ wells}$$

   This is to completely supersede the supply from
the catchment area, and using fairly comfortable
figure of consumption, which under the siege
conditions might be very considerably reduced.

   I am living at Pennant Hills - an unsewered
suburb, and our family of six adults is managing
to use on the average 31.2 gals. of water per day
per the whole family, and managing to be more
than reasonably clean. Thus about 5 gallons per
day per head is reasonable siege average, and
even 15 wells sunk in Botany would be ample to
provide the civilian population with minimum water
requirements.

   This number of wells could be sunk quickly
and equipped before the expected siege begins.
Connection to city mains should be made, and in this
case water shortage would not be responsible for
surrender.

There are scores of private wells drawing water
from Botany sands, and as soon as large scale offer
is made to use the underground supply of Botany for
public needs, the howl starts that only 8,000,000
gals. a day are available, and further draft will
destroy the existing private wells. This is not
so. The private owners will have to overhaul their
pumping plants, and lower their pump intakes with
the fall of pumping level.

The data on these private wells are very
contradictory and scarce. The above figure of
8,000,000 gals. was given in the press, but I doubt
its infallibility. All these private wells should
be investigated and entered on the map. The hourly
capacity of each well should be determined, as well
as the time it is operating daily. The static level
of water, and its drop under continuous pumping
should be indicated, as well as total depth of the
well, and the reduced level of its bottom referred
to the sea level.

The chemical and bacteriological tests of these
wells should be made, and if water is reasonably
clean and safe (very strict standards of the Water
Board will have to be probably reconsidered) -
connection with the public mains should be made.

The possible objection that the wells are
private, on private property - would not stand
criticism: first of all they are drawing God-sent
water, and secondly under the N.E.S. Regulations
private property might, and should be, commandeered
for the common good.

SUBURBS OTHER THAN BOTANY:
All restrictions on the provision of private
water supplies (which are illegal under the Act
which established the Water Board) should be lifted

immediately, and a propaganda campaign should
be launched in the press and over the wireless
recommending people to dig little conservation
dams, excavate shallow wells, or sink bores of
about 6" or less, and equip them with hand operated
pumps. This activity will indicate the state of
possible underground supplies and might lead to
bigger schemes. On a neighbouring property to ours
at Pennant Hills a water hole dug 10 ft. below the
ground level is yielding easily 50 gallons of water
per day.

  After being settled (and boiled for drinking)
this water will satisfy all domestic demands.

REGISTRATION OF WELL-SINKERS & EQUIPMENT:

  All people with experience in well sinking as
foremen and engineers, as well as all available
private and public plant for the well sinking should
be registered now and might be mobilised if not
otherwise made available.

STOP INCREASES IN SEWERED AREAS:

  For the duration of the war stop all increases in
the sewered areas. Sewered suburbs are using from
5-6 times more water than unsewered ones. Some of
the sewered suburbs might even be thrown back to
old-fashioned sanitary services to save water used
for flushing.

  In wealthier homes something between 10-15
gallons per day per head is being wasted by flushing
sanitary fixtures unnecessarily, as a matter of
habit.

WATER METERS:

  As far as the circumstances permit, attention
should be paid to the installation of water meters

for each individual consumer. Water rates should be
substituted by charges for water, and sliding scale
of these charges might regulate the consumption
during drought or emergency better than any appeals
to commonsense or patriotism of the general public.

In bringing the above to the notice of the
military command and civil Government, I hope that
the ideas exposed will be found useful, and if any
further considerations of such nature are required,
I should be only too glad to do all I can in the
result of about 40 years of experience in water
supply in Russia and China.

> Yours faithfully,
>
> (sgd.) J.A. YOUHOTSKY.[11]

INVASION - EVACUATION - SCORCHED EARTH?

One idea - defensive at that - cemented into millions of tons of concrete, into millions of minds of men, delivered France to complete defeat!

The disaster at Pearl Harbor derived from "Maginot-mindedness"!

A mental attitude to attack from the sea tucked an £135,000,000 naval base safely away in the narrow strait of Johore - for the Japanese to pluck by land!

The development of <u>one</u> defensive concept is sufficient to preoccupy the imagination, the labors, and the finances, of a generation: to tie armies and populations to its chariot wheels.

Yet prove worthless!

The Axis powers have conceived colossally over years, a Battle for Earth, using a Martian armoury, and a Brobdingnagian movement "to envelop-divide-destroy".

What we have treated as fiction, we have now too suddenly to confront - as fact!

We cannot meet it successfully by sending 20,000 fighting Australians to defend anachronistic fixations in Malaya.

Nor can we afford to indulge ourselves with any fixations in Australia.

There is breath-taking challenge today to previous standards.

x   x   x   x

The fact that we have radio-announced to Japan the intention to make Australia the allied base of a Pacific counter-offensive, constructed to deny to Nippon what it has so far conquered at cost, must quicken Japanese plans to clinch their Pacific victories by final conquest of the possibly final allied base.

If Nippon does attempt any invasion of Australia
at all, the attempt cannot be on less than a scale
computed to break through the Anzac Fleet, and to
succeed - as in Malaya, as in the Philippines, as
in -

And we can expect only the unexpected!

As at Pearl Harbor! As at Penang! As at Singapore!
As in Libya! As in the Straits of Dover!

But we do know by now the type and magnitude of
Axis war concepts: and we can imagine for ourselves
an Australian application.

Though it seek to envelop-divide-destroy, as
in Russia and in China, our Australian coast-wise
concentration and interior Egypt will give it a
geographical version kindred to Libya, edged with
Malaya!

The conquest of the territory from Maryborough,
Queensland, to Portland, Victoria, would be the
conquest of Australia.

The rest of Australia would count for little.
(Darwin belongs to the Java zone.)

Whilst we may mostly picture the Japanese in
the role of pearl fisher in northern Australian
waters, we must not forget that he was a woolbuyer
of Brisbane, Sydney and Melbourne, a diplomat of
Canberra - and an Antarctic whaler of consequence!

And that whaling launches, slid through the
hinged sides of whalers, make natural assault boats.

Among the Nipponese plans for the invasion of the
final allied base in the Pacific, there is no doubt
one resembling the following:

1. Three to four Macassar-sized convoys[12] - with
   balloon barrages, naval escort, and airplane
   "umbrellas". (The Pacific Ocean is wider than
   the Macassar Strait.)

2. Simultaneous major landings:
   (i)   South of Forster, N.S.W., outflanking the
           Port Stephens defences - with succeeding
           mechanised landings at the latter port.
   (ii)   Maryborough, Queensland.
   (iii)   Portland, Victoria.
3. Mechanised enveloping movements:
   (i)   Port Stephens north via Muswellbrook,
           the New England Highway and/or Inverell-
           Toowoomba to meet the Maryborough,
           Queensland, invading forces proceeding
           southerly through Kingaroy, Cooyar.
   (ii)   Muswellbrook west to Dubbo and southwards
           through Forbes to meet the northern
           advance of mechanised forces from
           Portland, Victoria, through Deniliquin-
           Narrandera (and the rice fields!)
4. Pincer movements on Melbourne, Canberra, Sydney
   and Brisbane - from the rear: supported by a
   secondary entry via Twofold Bay upon Canberra.
   Destruction of water supplies - e.g. Burrinjuck,
   Sydney &c.
5. Dividing movements - or retreats if necessary -
   from the Dividing Range down the west-east
   mountain roads to the coastal ports.
6. Naval and aerial actions along the coast in
   support.
7. Coastal infiltrations using coastal boats
   requisitioned from us.
8. Aerodrome captures.

This plan would call for 6,000,000 tons of
Japanese shipping - and a considerable part of the
Japanese navy. It is not likely to happen if Java
stands. If Java does not stand it could happen here!

x   x   x   x

Driven before the Japanese invaders, the Chinese
students of the Universities of Tientsin and Pekin

SINGAPORE

THEY grouped together about the chief,
  And each one looked at his mate,
Ashamed to think that Australian men
  Should meet such a bitter fate!
And black was the wrath in each hot heart,
  And savage oaths they swore,
As they thought of how they had all been ditched
  By "Impregnable" Singapore.

In her vaunted place she squatted the sea
  On a base that was Maginot bred,
Her startled face looked up at the skies
  To the enemy planes o'erhead.
Enemy planes while ours were—where?
  That cry we had heard before.
Our hearts were wrung as it rose this time
  From beleaguered Singapore.

She brought forth death as her eldest child,
  With defeat as her second son,
Then she hung a white flag out on a staff
  To show that her task was done;
And sick with rage the Australians stood,
  And God! how those Anzacs swore—
Bennett and all his men alike—
  At the fall of Singapore!

Whose was the fault she betrayed our troops?
  Whose was the fault she killed?
Ask it of those who lowered the flag
  That once to the mast was nailed!
Tell them we'll raise it on Anzac soil
  With hearts that are steeled to the core,
We swear by our dead and captive sons,
  REVENGE FOR SINGAPORE!

—MARY GILMORE

Propaganda poster from 1942 playing on fears of a Japanese invasion from the north.

THESE PLANES JOI

91/1 HIRO
Reconnaissance
(NAVY)

TYPE 97
Twin-Engined Flying Boat (NAVY)

KAWANISI
4-Engined Flying Boat
(NAVY)

MITSUBISHI
Single-Seater Fighter
(NAVY)

AICHI A-1 104
Floatplane Bomber
(NAVY)

MITSUBISHI
Single-Seater Fighter
(NAVY)

MITSUBISHI
Dive-Bomber
(NAVY)

NAKAJIMA NAKA 93
Floatplane Fighter
(NAVY)

KAWANISI
Reconnaissance Floatplane
(NAVY)

MITSUBISHI
Light-Bomber
(ARMY)

Virgil

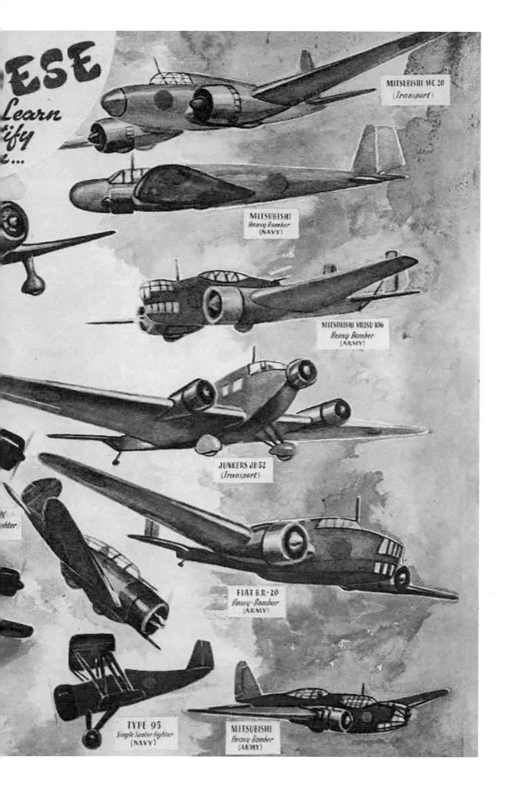

ESE

Learn
tify
...

MITSUBISHI MC 20
(Transport)

MITSUBISHI
Heavy Bomber
(NAVY)

MITSUBISHI MITSU 106
Heavy Bomber
(ARMY)

JUNKERS JU 52
(Transport)

FIAT B.R.-20
Heavy Bomber
(ARMY)

TYPE 95
Single Seater Fighter
(NAVY)

MITSUBISHI
Heavy Bomber
(ARMY)

Poster, issued by the Beaufort Anti Waste campaign, showing Melbourne's Flinders Street Station under Japanese occupation.

FASHION PORTFOLIO

Prepared to be useful . . .

● Fetching dirndl style interpreted in white cotton overchecked in red and blue. The trim, shirtwaist bodice is contrasted by a swing skirt, garnished with two huge pockets and disciplined at the waist with a drawstring. (Right.)

+ + +

● For digging in the vegetable patch, waist-waisted overalls in royal-blue cotton are worn with a workmanlike shirt in red and white stripes and curls are swept up into a matching mammy handkerchief. (Below.)

● Practical and pretty is this trim knoppe linen pinafore in stop-red, enhanced with a youthful white cotton blouse coin-spotted in green.

● Ready for a hard day's work in dark brown overall culottes with two capacious pockets. With it a pastel-blue blouse and mustard straw hat.

RENÉ

Wartime fashions shifted to the utilitarian as part of an overall shift to practicality.

Recycling of rubber products for the manufacture of tyres and other military uses was one of many recycling programs, aluminium being another.

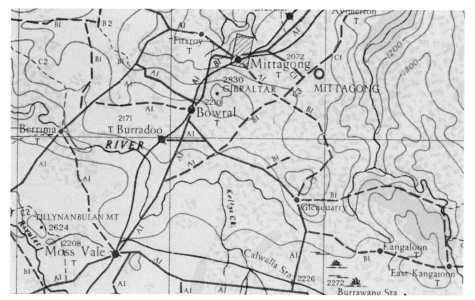

THIS MAP IS AN OFFICIAL DOCUMENT. IF FOUND, IT MUST BE HANDED IN TO THE
NEAREST MILITARY HEADQUARTERS OR POLICE STATION

Roads Concrete or sealed			———
Roads Metal or gravel			– – – –
Roads or Tracks Earth			·········
Width sufficient for	two traffic streams	A	
	one traffic stream with occasional passing	B	
	one traffic stream only	C	
Suitable for	Heavy M.T.	1	
	Light M.T. (up to 3 ton lorries)	2	
	Horse transport only	3	
	Pack transport only	4	
Note: Brackets denote wet weather classification		B2(C3)	

Telephone line along Road	·—·—·—
High Tension Power line	H.T.L.
Electric Power Station — Main	▭
Terminal Sub-station	◪
Municipal or Private	○
Railway and Railway Station	━━━
Railway Station with Siding	━◆━
Railway Siding	————
Aerodrome, A or A1 Class	◉
Aerodrome, B Class	○
Aerodrome, C Class or Emergency Landing Ground	◒
Seaplane Base	⚓
Seaplane mooring area	⚓

Part of a larger Wollongong area map prepared by the Army's Cartographic
Corps and used by military planners, showing access routes, dams, waterways,
utilities and transport.

The Beaufort Bomber was produced at Port Melbourne by the Department of Aircraft. It was a high-performance aircraft first flown in Australia in August 1941.

took their books and appliances, the factory workers
their tools and machinery, the merchants their
ledgers and abaci, the peasants their household
goods - and these, in their millions and mostly
afoot, jog trotted over three thousand miles of dirt
tracks to a New China of which Chungking became the
capital, and the Burma Road its only lane of warlike
supply.

At Russian injunction, the <u>evacuating</u> Chinese
left behind them their good earth scorched to
desert - as a barrier to Nippon.

In vast Russia, Stalin's men lured Hitler's hosts
into the winter snows that had beaten Napoleon,
and smashed their own industrial gods to interpose
between themselves and the Germans a no-man's land
of scorched earth and guerilla "islands": to cheat
the invader of wanted resources, to compel him to
painfully transport from his own reserves, his
own means of supply, to harry his communications,
to leave "pools" of guerillas to join with the
readvancing "floods" of armies when the Russians
marched again.

In Malaya, the Japanese lived on the country;
and requisitioning parties followed closely the
infiltrating parties. Malaya, Burma, and the Dutch
East Indies contain 80% of the world's rubber, 70%
of the tin, much of the petroleum. After Penang, we
realised that what had to be abandoned of these war-
stores must be first destroyed so that the enemy
might not gain to his use what the democracies had
lost to theirs.

In Australia, we must not let ourselves become
either Maginot-minded - or Penang-minded!

But we cannot retreat from our zones of dense
population to found a new Australia and find a
new Sydney-Brisbane-Melbourne-Canberra at Alice

Springs. Nor can we transfer our people beyond Urals
we do not possess. Nor have we rubber, or petroleum,
of which we must deprive the enemy at all costs.

There is danger in emulation: if our case be
different!

Because other countries have found reason for
a policy of scorched earth is not necessarily in
itself reason for its adoption for Australia.

If our strategy does not propose evacuation,
it has no "scorched earth" policy to implement!
"Scorched earth" is corollary to the military
evacuation of a countryside under irresistible
military pressure, directly or indirectly applied.
Unless such an evacuation includes the producing
forces and their domestic auxiliary, "scorched
earth" in the Chinese-Russian sense, does not make
sense here.

If we determine to stand and fight to the last
man, to fortify our cities and industries, to fight
house by house and street by street, our evacuation-
plus-scorched earth tactic will be a limited
salvage-plus-demolition process.

If we are involved in a Japanese invasion plan
such as that hypothecated for the purpose of this
mental exercise, our evacuation-plus-scorched
earth tactic will also be a limited salvage-plus-
demolition process because we shall retire to
defensible refuges in the ranges, the Russian
"island" defence tactic, whence we can harry enemy
communications, and re-integrate in a new advance.

If we must act upon the defensive, the
initiative will be the enemy's. He will determine
our evacuations, if any, and their accompanying
"scorched earth" operations.

Of his strategy we shall not be told until the
unexpected happens. We must, therefore, so organise

that at any place at any time we must have a plan of
retirement in any direction, and a plan of instant
salvage and demolition which will retain for us, in
withdrawal, all possible essential stores, leaving
nothing for the use of enemy occupying forces.

And certainly no fishing boats or coastal
shipping for his use in coastal infiltrations.

And as certainly no motor vehicles and no petrol.

And as little water and food as possible.

We should not hesitate to sacrifice our
Dnieperpetrovsk dams if it pays militarily so to
do - but the military profit and loss of civil
destructions must be coldly calculated before the
military button is finally pressed.

And since the fighting forces will be busy
fighting for us - and dying for us - Civil
Collaboration must be organised everywhere to
instant-automatic "scorched earth" evacuations to
plan when that button is pressed - leaving only to
the hard-pressed fighting forces the final military
demolitions of retreat.

There is plenty of Australia from which we could
evacuate without danger of defeat - but these places
will not interest the enemy.

There are places in Australia from which we
must not retreat. These are Sydney and Newcastle,
Melbourne, Brisbane and Canberra.

And these places will interest the enemy.

They must be fortified: the sandbagged buildings
must be used not only as air-raid shelters!

They are our Leningrads and Moscows.

Four hundred thousand Japanese soldiers must not
be allowed to conquer seven million Australian men,
women, and children.

Nor can they - if we organise Civil Collaboration:
as in Russia! As in China!

If we incorporate Civil Collaboration as a
military measure of modern warfare, not only are our
defensive operations consolidated at their weakest
point, but some part of our defending forces could
be released to take the offensive towards Java.

If not, we remain upon the defensive awaiting our
turn for invasion.

The defensive does not pay in the long run. It
must evolve to the offensive which provides the
initiative to victory.

Let us have Total Organisation!

TOTAL ORGANISATION -

National war-time policies, through -

(i)   Limitation of civil supply - by import
        cessation, reduction of "non-essential"
        industry, rationing, rationalisation, and
        economic concentration.

(ii)   National Service operations - by conscriptive
        diversion of human-power to war -

are processing to reduce the citizen structure to -

(i)   The Fighting Arm.

(ii)   The Production Arm.

(iii)   The Cadet Arm.

(iv)   The Domestic Arm.

The Cadet Arm will consist of boys and girls between
13-18. It represents future reinforcements-in-
training for the Fighting and Production Arms.

The Domestic Arm excludes all persons in the home
engaged in the first three Arms. It has two sections:

(i)   Auxiliary to the Production Arm - the homes
        and domestic associates of the essential
        worker.

(ii)   Unattached - (a) the non-working wives and
                         children of soldiers and
                         sailors.

                     (b) the non-working aged
                         unfit, widows, children.

The unattached section of the Domestic Arm can be:

(a) Transferred to relieve congestion in danger
    areas; and/or

(b) Organised to voluntary aid, camouflage netting,
    care of unfit, aged and young &c.

The Auxiliary section of the Domestic Arm (auxiliary
to the Production Arm) should ordinarily stay at its

post - but may be permitted voluntary transfer from
danger areas where the safety of children (under 13-
14) is involved.

The Cadet Arm should be mobilised at base camps in
"safe" areas for combined vocational and military
training (including parachute tower exercises). The
Armidale University College could be used as a base
for the technical-professional group.

Note: The word "evacuation" should not be used
       in these connections: it is a military term
       meaning "to withdraw from a city or fortress"
       implying total abandonment: it conveys a
       sense of flight, and produces a psychological
       unease and a mental and emotional confusion
       which may become a defeatist morale - a sauve
       qui peut complex.
       There can be no evacuation except by force
       of the enemy - but there can be a war-time
       redistribution of population and industry,
       a civil mobilisation, a marshalling of the
       total community to total battle.

If we implement the above war logic, we have left in
the battle zones:
(i)   The Fighting Arm.
(ii)   The Production Arm - with its auxiliary
       Domestic Arm.

The Production Arm (and its auxiliary domestic)
should become corporate with the Fighting Arm before
battle (since battle will compel its involuntary and
unorganised incorporation anyhow - vide Singapore).

The war functions of the Production Arm (with its
Auxiliary Domestic) must be:

(i)   Essential administration, service and
        industry - up to front line.

(ii)   Self-defence against air attack and
        incendiarism (A.R.P.-N.E.S.).

(iii)   Self-salvage and self-demolition in military
        emergency.

(iv)   Self-transport and self-retreat in
        emergency.

(v)   Self-defence and self-fortification against
        enemy infiltration, parachute troops, street
        fighting, (V.D.C.).

(vi)   Self first-aid.

(vii)   Self-planning to guiding principles
        militarily enunciated in the Master Plan for
        Citizen Collaboration.

Note: The civil structure is too complex,
        subdivided and immobile for direct military
        incorporation. Nor can it be directly
        commanded. Incorporation and command,
        therefore, will have to be indirect - viz. via
        a Master Plan enlisting each unit organisation
        to a general scheme of civil collaboration on
        lines (i) to (vii). Military direction will
        be given by military revision of the Plan,
        and by delegating to the State War Effort Co-
        Ordination Committees the responsibility of
        implementing the militarily approved Plan.

Each staff of each essential administration service
and industry, therefore, should be enrolled as -

            AN INDUSTRIAL V.D.C. (= C.C.C.).

officered by its own management, planning its war
functions (i-vii) for itself but in conformity with

the Master C.C.C. Plan, and with responsibility
of the Management to the War Effort Co-ordination
Committee for approval and supervision, in
accordance with the militarily-endorsed Master
C.C.C. Plan.

For convenience, this type of organisation is
named the "Civil Collaboration Column"; in itself
it is unarmed, <u>but a volunteer section of each</u>
<u>industrial C.C.C. should be enlisted as a V.D.C.</u>
<u>section to act as guard to it</u>, and to combine in
emergency with the V.D.C. sections of neighbouring
C.C.C. industrial detachments into a guard for
a street block or defined locality under an Area
Leader, with its own casualty clearing station.

This type of organisation should reconcile both
the military concept and the emotional urge of the
Reserved Occupations (expressed in demands for a
Peoples' Army &c), for more direct participation in
defence.

It would:

(i)   Ensure instant-automatic civil collaboration
        with military strategy and tactic in
        emergency, and relieve the military general
        staff of civil dead weight.

(ii)   Use the part-time energies of the civil
        worker where they can best be organised and
        applied.

(iii)   Satisfy the psychological need of the
        reserved worker for self-approved warlike
        activity; inspire a corporate aggressive
        morale; and harness industrial energy to the
        war machine.

(iv)   Produce a degree of mobility and self-defence
        in the civil structure and make each building
        a fortified post.

(v)   Call upon each unit-organisation for self-finance, with appropriate tax rebate.

(vi)   Require after-hours drill; support of National Emergency regulation, and supervisory control by the War Effort Co-ordination Committee to make it effective.

Waste not Want not

Has always been a good maxim and is most applicable to our present conditions. Arnott's Biscuits can be eaten with a minimum of waste. They are ready without preparation and full of nourishment.

Our Milk Arrowroot, Shredded Wheatmeal, Milk Coffee, Sao, Digestive, Butter Oat Cakes, and many other lines can all be recommended as good foods at any time of the day.

Care should be taken to keep the lids closed down when tins are not in use.

SHREDDED WHEATMEAL

DIGESTIVE

WHEAT LUNCH

BUTTER OAT CAKE

Lend to Defend

Arnott's
FAMOUS
BISCUITS

WILLIAM ARNOTT PTY. LIMITED, HOMEBUSH.

PLEASE RETURN ALL EMPTY TINS TO YOUR GROCER AS SOON AS POSSIBLE

2

THE SCORCHED EARTH CODE

The first draft of the NSW Scorched Earth Code was distributed for comment in early April 1942, just over six weeks after the Swain subcommittee's first meeting. In that time, the subcommittee, with input from the military and state government officials, had refined Swain's document, 'Total War and Total Citizen Collaboration', to produce the Scorched Earth Code. The Code was divided into two components, the General Citizen Code and the Industrial and Services Code. These were covered in more detail in separate documents (reproduced in chapters 3 and 4).

The summarised Code reproduced here set out a prioritised list of the public and industrial resources that must be denied to the enemy; the agency or department responsible for them; the local entity that would carry out the denial; and the means of denial—explosives, fire and axe, scuttling, smashing, and so on. The highest priority for denial was given to resources in country areas outside the industrial strip from Newcastle through Sydney to Port Kembla.

The summary also considered resources held by individual citizens that might also aid the enemy. These included small watercraft, motor vehicles, binoculars and cameras, maps, batteries, tents, horses, saddles, first aid kits, food, boots and blankets. Like the larger resources, these were to be destroyed at the last minute, but the task of doing so would have to be entrusted to the owners—some of whom would find it difficult or impossible to follow through. Destruction was to be 'Simple, Silent, Selective, Swift'. Wherever possible, objects were to be first smashed or disabled, then burned or blown up.

The population of an invaded area was to disperse before military operations began and not return unless ordered by the military. This was to ensure that operations were not impeded by the movement of civilians.

THE SCORCHED EARTH CODE.

ø/ Scorched Earth Strategy.

ø/ Category of Denials in Services and Industries.

ø/ Citizen Possessions and Responsibilities.

ø/ The Citizen's Role.

ø/ Support Squads - as Citizen Aids.

ø/ War Damage and Scorched Earth Insurance.

ø/ National Security Regulations and Military
Powers.

ø/ Dispersal and Disposal First!

ø/ Destruction - simple, silent, selective, swift!

ø/ Scorched Earth Codes:

GENERAL CITIZEN CODE.

INDUSTRIAL AND SERVICES CODE.

SCORCHED EARTH STRATEGY AND PURPOSES:

The purposes of Scorched Earth operations are:

ø/ To prevent the enemy living on the country,
and using our property against us.

ø/ To force him to use his own precious
shipping, to deplete his own country of
supplies, to sustain and maintain his own
armies.

ø/ To attack him, through fire and destruction.

ø/ To obstruct and to impede him, and dislodge
his foothold.

ø/ To slow up his advance.

ø/ To leave him nothing to loot and remove to
his own country.

ø/ To deny him everything in our country.

Either we employ Scorched Earth against the
enemy - or he uses it against us!

We have to face up to a Scorched Earth Policy
as the Russians did at Dnepropetrovsk Dam[1] and
elsewhere; as the Chinese did in China.

We can't mix Peace and War!

We are at Total War!

We can build again - and better - when we have thrown the last Japanese into the Pacific.

Scorched Earth is a counter offensive.

It requires ruthless resolution and aggression.

Category of Priorities in Services and Industries:

Although Scorched Earth operations may be ruthless, they must he calculated; military and civil reasons are given here; military control must be maintained - lest unwanted and wanton destruction occur.

To be most effective, a Scorched Earth policy must be selective.

It must be applied thoroughly at all key points from which the enemy can derive benefit, and to that which he most needs and has greatest difficulty in replacing.

At military discretion, it can be applied also in the first, second, or third degree, viz:

First degree - Tactical demolitions.

Second degree - Parched Earth destruction.

Third degree - Scorched Earth destruction.

The first degree relates to such things as jetties, bridges, railways, roads, telegraphs &c. The second extends to oil wells and oil supplies, coastal craft, motor vehicles, foodstuffs and other things of early use to the enemy. The third degree extends to everything!

Here is a category of our resources, arranged in order of likely enemy use:

SCORCHED EARTH CATEGORY.

(Listing resources in general order of denial value for selective demolition – subject to all possible prior dispersal, disposal or salvage.)

Resource Groups.	Supervising Agency for State War Effort Co-ordination Committee Scorched Earth Operational Plans.	Local Agency for Action Detail operations and execution.	Denial Methods Abridged (see Unit Codes).
A. Landing facilities (exclusive of those between Port Stephens and Port Kembla):			
(i) Ocean jetties wharves, bunkers &c.	Public Works Dept.	Local Public Works Dept. staff.	Explosives.
(ii) Estuary jetties, wharves, bunkers etc.	Public Works Dept. and affected Shires.	Local Public Works Dept. and Shire Staffs.	Fire and axe.
B. Coastwise infiltration facilities:			

Resource Groups.	Supervising Agency for State War Effort Co-ordination Committee Scorched Earth Operational Plans.	Local Agency for Action Detail operations and execution.	Denial Methods Abridged (see Unit Codes).
(i) Pleasure and non-essential boats and watercraft.	Maritime Services Board – Fisheries (in collaboration with the Navy up to the mooring point or thereafter with the Army).	Local Fisheries Inspectors and Maritime Services Bd. officers – with boatmen crews.	Mooring at heads of rivers, with subsequent salvaging of engines &c. and scuttling or burning in emergency.
(ii) Economically essential boats and watercraft.			

C. Public Transport Systems:

(i) Railways and rolling stock, repair shops.	Department of Railways.	Railway staff.	Special action detail.
(ii) Roads, road bridges and crossings, road-making plant and equipment.	Department of Main Roads.	Local Main Roads and Shire staff.	Explosives, fire and axe.

D. Motor Fuels:

Resource Groups.	Supervising Agency for State War Effort Co-ordination Committee Scorched Earth Operational Plans.	Local Agency for Action Detail operations and execution.	Denial Methods Abridged (see Unit Codes).
(i) Petrol, diesel fuels, oils, greases, kerosene, power alcohol.	Defence Forces	Defence Forces' Personnel.	Running to waste; firing as a last resort.
(ii) Charcoal.	State Charcoal Production Management.	Local staffs.	Burning and scattering.
E. Motor & other Transport:			
Cars, trucks lorries, trailers.	Department of Road Transport.	Citizen owner or user.	Removing & smashing essential working parts.
Tractors.			Running to seize up.
Tyres.			Slashing, burning.
Batteries.			Smashing.
Tools and accessories.			Burying, throwing in deep water.
Buses.	Department of Road Transport.	Department of Road Transport.	Special action detail.

Resource Groups.	Supervising Agency for State War Effort	Local Agency for Action	Denial Methods
	Co-ordination Committee Scorched Earth Operational Plans.	Detail operations and execution.	Abridged (see Unit Codes).
Bicycles.	Scorched Earth Support Squads, and Local Government Authorities.	Citizen owner or user.	Smashing wheels and forks.
Waggons, drays, sulkies, buggies. Horses.	"	"	Smashing wheels, burning. Shooting.
F. Repair Equipment and Replacements: Spare parts and accessories.	Scorched Earth Support Squads, and	Proprietors or Managers & Staffs of Garages,	Smashing, burying.
Trade and ordinary tools. Workshop equipment.	Local Govt. Authorities and Trade Groups	Engineering and Blacksmiths' shops and stores.	Destroying power plant, essential tools, parts and machines.
G. Communication Systems:			

UNITY MEANS VICTORY

AUSTRALIA SHALL NOT FALL

A Call to Action

We can, and we will, beat the Japanese. If they come to Australia, we can beat them in Australia, and we can beat them out of it.

What are the Japanese? They are brave men; they are intelligent men, but they are no more than men.

They have unity. They have the spirit of self-sacrifice. They have good organisation, founded on hard work, attention to detail, and bold and original ideas. They have capable and courageous leaders imbued with the offensive spirit.

Bennett's brigades had all these things, and Bennett's brigades showed that they could beat them.

We can have all these things here in Australia, because we are Australians, like Bennett's men—like the A.I.F. in Greece. We have them in our own hearts and minds and bodies. If we bring them out and use them, we shall win.

IT looks as if the period of waiting and wondering is at an end. In a few weeks, we shall probably be into the crisis, perhaps we shall be through it. To any man of courage, that should bring a feeling of relief, almost of exaltation.

But it means, above all, that every hour of our time not given directly to the war effort is another ounce in the scales on Japan's side.

What about unity, in the first place? If unity means anything, it means laying aside differences and disputes which were, perhaps, all important when the war was no closer than Libya.

MR. CURTIN

Mr. Curtin is Prime Minister. He is a man, unambitious, but high-principled, of considerable ability, stronger and more decisive than his quiet manner suggests, anxious to give any matter a calm and judicial decision, and, above all, determined to win the war for his country and for humanity. We could not choose a better leader to-day.

For us there are no more parties; Mr. Curtin is Australia's leader.

Mr. Curtin has various Ministers. Some of them are efficient, others are not.

If Mr. Curtin can strengthen his team at short notice, well and good. If he does not, they are entitled, every one of them, to the undiluted loyalty, co-operation, and constructive assistance of every citizen to the utmost.

THE PARTY GAME

With too many of us, party politics is still being played. There are men who think that no good can ever come out of Labour, there are many who, if the Minister's way is not theirs, if they suffer hardship or injustice, feel justified in holding back a little.

Let them keep their troubles until afterwards. The only "fair share" is the utmost they can do.

There are men on the Labour side, both in politics and in the unions, deeply suspicious of the industrialists and of big business, also holding back, lest their rights be endangered.

There are no rights worth a damn until we have beaten the Japanese.

The time has come to stop prating about privileges, money, rights, wages, profits, or anything else. We know well enough how conquered countries are treated.

If a man comes out of this war with a whole skin, with his wife and family safe, and with the capacity to earn an honest living, he should fall down on his knees and thank God, and there are many who will thank Him for less than that.

You may see the man next to you loafing, making a good thing out of the war, doing you out of something. But don't stop to argue now. Curse him under your breath, get on with your own job, and deal with him afterwards.

DUTY OF THE PRESS

The main job of the Press in war-time is to see that people know as much as possible of the truth of what is happening all over the world. Telling the truth in the news columns and in comment involves showing up mistakes.

The "Herald" has never been more searching or more unsparing than during the war; we have probably trodden on every corn both in the Empire and outside it. Why? Because failure means death and destruction.

GET ON WITH THE JOB NOW

IT is therefore with all the more force that we appeal to you in this vital moment: Follow the leaders you have and get on with the job. Make the best of the existing organisation; support it, help it, work with it.

No one knows better than we do where there are still faults. If they can be cured at short notice, let us get to it. If they can't, let us stop moaning and wait until we have more breathing space.

Never mind now what Britain or America did or failed to do. They have a free Press there, which is rapidly waking up to say all that we have said or might say at this juncture. If they can't cure their own faults, well—

The enemy makes mistakes, too.

You will notice all around you cases where this or that need has been insufficiently organised or provided for. A month ago it was still a good idea to write to the papers or organise deputations to the Minister. Now the thing to do is to do something about it yourself.

ACT FOR YOURSELF

If it is air-raid shelters, collect your friends and go and dig trenches. If it is fire-fighting or first aid, go and find out how to act yourself. There are books you can get, other people who know; go and look for them.

If you are in an area which could be invaded, don't gird now at the Government for not having done more about guerilla warfare or scorched earth. Think things out for yourself,

see the police and the local authorities, read the papers, where these matters have been explained.

Then, if the worst happens, do your best. You do not need a shotgun. You can destroy or deny the enemy facilities and supplies and materials they will want.

In short, where Australian organisation has slipped, improvise it with Australian initiative, resourcefulness and team work. This applies with especial force if you are in the Government, or any public service, or even the Services. If things are not being done, get them done somehow; risk being sacked or reprimanded afterwards.

If you are on leave, don't get drunk to-night, you may be needed to-morrow.

OUR STRENGTH IS GROWING FAST

WE have said we could, and we would, beat the Japanese. The Australian militia alone ought to beat a stronger force than the Japanese ever had in Malaya.

And they will not be alone. We have American help; and we have commanders, both Americans and Australians, who are world-beaters.

Moreover, every week that goes by sees better training, more equipment from our own factories, which are turning out good material, and in good quantities.

It is impossible to speak openly about the naval and air position. But talk of "hello coming" need not raise scornful recollections of Java, Malaya, Greece, and so on. There is quite enough here already to hit hard, and help is coming by a much safer route than it did to Java or Malaya.

JAPAN'S LOSSES

At sea, the Achilles heel of Japan is cruisers. Having 35 to 40 to start with, she has about half that number sunk or out of action with heavy damage; and cruisers are the backbone of any fleet unit. She can, and will, spare considerable forces for us. But the risk is getting greater, and the margin of permissible losses, with the main American fleet not yet in action, is getting pretty small.

It is amazing to go about Sydney and hear some intelligent and level-headed people, dazed by the Japanese successes, talk as if we had about a fifty-fifty chance. We have a right to feel as Britain felt on the eve, as thought, of German invasion.

As in Britain, our defences are not yet perfected. As in Britain, they are improving every day. Faced with a united people who took the stand that defeat was inconceivable, the Germans were astonished and abashed. They were beaten in the air, they went no further.

NO "SAFE PLACE"

The hardest thing for us, as a civilised people, to realise is that this war has to be fought with the lives of our women and children, as well as of our men. The country's safety must be put above everyone's.

If invasion comes, there is no "safe place" to send anyone to. We cannot repeat the dreadful tale of refugees blocking roads in France. The only safety is in victory.

This is not just an ordinary war of conquest like the Great War, the Napoleonic War, or any of the wars of recent history. The Nazis have changed all that.

Inflamed by a new religion of darkness and brutality, they have swept down upon a peaceful and luxury-loving world as

the Goths and Vandals did upon ancient Rome. Civilisation has reached its greatest crisis since the fall of the Roman Empire. For what is civilisation? It has nothing to do with a knowledge of chemistry or science. It is a thing of the mind, of the spirit. It is a question of right and wrong, a question of whether you can behave in a civilised manner.

If a man spreads fire and destruction, hatred and murder through the world, he is a barbarian as surely as was Attila the Hun, and his victory will assuredly plunge the world back into the gloom of primitive savagery.

A HITLER ALLY

Even if they were not attacking Australia, it would be enough for us that the Japanese are fighting on Hitler's side.

There are times when Australians don't know their own strength, won't use their own strength; waste it in fighting each other. We will use it, of course, when we think the fight is on.

But that is too late. We must use it now. The fight is on.

JOHN FAIRFAX & SONS
PTY. LTD.
Proprietors,
"THE SYDNEY MORNING HERALD"

Resource Groups.	Supervising Agency for State War Effort Co-ordination Committee Scorched Earth Operational Plans.	Local Agency for Action Detail operations and execution.	Denial Methods Abridged (see Unit Codes).
Transmitting Stations	Postmaster General's Dept.	Broadcasting Station management staff.	Special action detail.
Telegraph & Telephone Exchanges and Systems: Postmaster General's.	Postmaster General's Dept.	Post & Telegraph staffs, supervisors &c. Exchange staffs, supervisors &c.	Special action detail.
Railway.	Department of Railways.	Railway staff.	"
Wireless receiving sets – battery and electric.	Scorched Earth Support Squads & Local Govt. Authorities.	The citizen owner or user.	Smashing valves, transformers and essential parts.
H. Coal Stocks and Mines: Colliery pit heads, installations and machinery	Department of Mines.	Colliery Management and Staffs.	Special action detail.

Resource Groups.	Supervising Agency for State War Effort Co-ordination Committee Scorched Earth Operational Plans.	Local Agency for Action Detail operations and execution.	Denial Methods Abridged (see Unit Codes).
I. Industrial Stocks: <u>At Factories,</u> <u>Wholesalers,</u> <u>Retailers:</u> Coal, fuels, charcoal, timber	Scorched Earth Support Squads, Local Govt. Authorities & Industrial and Trade Groups.	Industrial management & staffs, or Citizen owner.	Burning.
Raw materials, manufactured articles, food and especially spirits, beers, wines & salt.	"	"	Smashing, burning, burying, throwing into deep water, running to waste and dispersing.
J. <u>Household</u> <u>foodstuffs, spirits,</u> <u>beer, wines, salt,</u> <u>clothing, tools,</u> <u>wireless sets,</u> <u>telephones:</u>	Scorched Earth Support Squads & Local Govt. Authorities.	The Citizen owner or user.	Smashing, burning, burying, throwing into deep water, running to waste and dispersing.

Resource Groups.	Supervising Agency for State War Effort Co-ordination Committee Scorched Earth Operational Plans.	Local Agency for Action Detail operations and execution.	Denial Methods Abridged (see Unit Codes).
<u>Supplies of Water:</u> Tanks, wells, dams, windmills, pipes, pumps.	Scorched Earth Support Squads and Local Government Authorities.	The Citizen Owner or User.	Running to waste, puncturing, smashing.
K. <u>Bulk Wool</u> <u>Bulk Flour</u> <u>Bulk Grain and Cereals (Rice, Wheat, Maize &c.)</u>			
At wool stores and woollen mills:	N.S.W. Wool Committee.	Management & staffs of wool stores and woollen mills.	Special action detail.
At flour mills:	Dept. of Agriculture.	Mill & management staffs.	Special action detail.
At grain silos & stacks:	Dept. of Agriculture.	Grain Elevator Staffs.	Special action detail.

Resource Groups.	Supervising Agency for State War Effort Co-ordination Committee Scorched Earth Operational Plans.	Local Agency for Action Detail operations and execution.	Denial Methods Abridged (see Unit Codes).
L. Farmers & Graziers' Stock and Produce. <u>Fodder:</u> Growing crops, haystacks, ensilage. Rice crops.	Scorched Earth Support Squads & Local Govt. Authorities.	The farmer and grazier owner	Mowing, drying & firing. Draining water from green rice crops; burning ripe rice crops.
<u>Stock:</u> Horses, cattle, pigs, poultry.		"	Slaughtering.
<u>Cereals & Grain</u> <u>Stocks:</u> Wheat, rice, maize &c.		"	Scattering or soaking with water.

Resource Groups.	Supervising Agency for State War Effort Co-ordination Committee Scorched Earth Operational Plans.	Local Agency for Action Detail operations and execution.	Denial Methods Abridged (see Unit Codes).
M. Forests and Bush Timber Depots.	Forestry Commission.	Forestry Commission's staff & citizen owners.	Fire.
N. Primary Production: Equipment: Pastoral and farming machinery and implements.	Scorched Earth Support Squads & Local Govt. Authorities.	Farmer or grazier owner or user.	Breaking wheels and working parts; removing and burying tines, shares, discs &c. Smashing power plant.
O. Installations: Electric light & power generating and distributing plants and stations.	Public Works Department.	County Councils' Staffs.	Special action detail.
Gas supply.	Local Government Dept.	Municipal Councils and Gas Companies' staffs.	Special action detail.

Resource Groups.	Supervising Agency for State War Effort	Local Agency for Action	Denial Methods
	Co-ordination Committee Scorched Earth Operational Plans.	Detail operations and execution.	Abridged (see Unit Codes).
Water Storage and Reticulation.	Metropolitan Water Sewerage & Drainage Board. Water Conservation & Irrigation Commission.	Water Board's, Irrigation's, and Municipal & Shire Councils' staffs.	Special action detail.
P. Manufacturing & Industrial: (a) General Plant & Machinery: Machine tools. Power Units. Welding plants. Furnaces. Compressors. Precision tools and gauges.	Scorched Earth Support Squads and Industrial & Trade Groups.	Factory and workshop management and staffs.	See Industrial Code for detailed methods of denial.

Resource Groups.	Supervising Agency for State War Effort	Local Agency for Action	Denial Methods
	Co-ordination Committee Scorched Earth Operational Plans.	Detail operations and execution.	Abridged (see Unit Codes).
(b) Particular Plant Machinery and Materials:			
(1) Metal Industries and General Engineering.			
Agricultural implement Manufacture.			
Aluminium manufacture.			
Brass and bronze manufacture.			
Electro-plating.			
Engineering, foundry and boiler making.			
Farriers and blacksmiths.			
Fences and gate manufacture.			

Resource Groups.	Supervising Agency for State War Effort	Local Agency for Action	Denial Methods
	Co-ordination Committee Scorched Earth Operational Plans.	Detail operations and execution.	Abridged (see Unit Codes).
Galvanising works. Iron and steel production. Machinery manufacture. Mining and ore treatment plants. Motor industry. Nails, barbed wire, bolts and nuts. Nickelware manufacture. Plumbing and hot water engineering. Refrigeration. Repair equipment – garage and general. Sawmills. Spring makers. Ship Builders.	Scorched Earth Support Squads and Industrial & Trade Groups.	Factory and workshop management and staffs.	See Industrial Code for detailed methods of denial.

Resource Groups.	Supervising Agency for State War Effort Co-ordination Committee Scorched Earth Operational Plans.	Local Agency for Action Detail operations and execution.	Denial Methods Abridged (see Unit Codes).
Tin smiths and sheet metal works.			
Tool making.			
Wire rope.			
Wire drawers.			
2. Precision Instruments:			
Opticians and watchmakers.			
Scientific instrument makers.			
Surgical instrument makers.			
Survey instrument makers.			
3. Chemical Industries:			
Oil refining and distribution.			
Explosive manufacture.			

Resource Groups.	Supervising Agency for State War Effort	Local Agency for Action	Denial Methods
	Co-ordination Committee Scorched Earth Operational Plans.	Detail operations and execution.	Abridged (see Unit Codes).
Glue, glycerine and soap factories. Dry battery manufacture. Acid manufacture. Arsenic production and refining. Photographic apparatus and materials. Pharmaceutical, chemical manufactures. Optical glass manufacture and assembly plants. Paint and varnish factories. 4. Electrical Industries:	Scorched Earth Support Squads and Industrial & Trade Groups.	Factory and workshop management and staffs.	See Industrial Code for detailed methods of denial.

Resource Groups.	Supervising Agency for State War Effort	Local Agency for Action	Denial Methods Abridged (see Unit Codes).
	Co-ordination Committee Scorched Earth Operational Plans.	Detail operations and execution.	
Accumulator and battery makers.			
Electrical machinery and apparatus.			
Insulation manufacture.			
5. Foodstuff industries:			
Breweries.			
Distilleries.			
Wine industries.			
Flour and rice mills.			
Abbatoirs and butcheries.			
Dairy produce factories.			
Canneries.			
Sugar refineries.			

Resource Groups.	Supervising Agency for State War Effort	Local Agency for Action	Denial Methods
	Co-ordination Committee Scorched Earth Operational Plans.	Detail operations and execution.	Abridged (see Unit Codes).
6. Textile and Leather Industries:	Scorched Earth Support Squads and Industrial & Trade Groups.	Factory and workshop management and staffs.	See Industrial Code for detailed methods of denial.

Boot factories.
Tents, sails and canvas goods.
Woollen, cotton, weaving & knitwear industries.
Ropes and twines.
Leather trades – general.
Water proof and gasproof materials.
Paper manufacture.

NOTE: FIRST ATTENTION SHOULD BE PAID TO COUNTRY UNITS OUTSIDE THE INDUSTRIAL CENTRES OF NEWCASTLE, SYDNEY and PORT KEMBLA, PARTICULARLY THOSE ON THE COAST.

A warden uncovers an unexploded shell after the shelling of
Sydney on 8 June 1942.

Against each item is given the authority, owner or user; who will be required:

(i)   To prepare at once an effective plan of destruction.

(ii)   To prepare at once complete working arrangements for demolition.

(iii)   To train and rehearse existing staff so that they are ready to ruthlessly demolish at a moment's notice.

(iv)   As civil soldiers, to carry out the military order instantly it is received.

(v)   To stick to their civil posts until the job is done; that is, until the enemy is denied the use of the item.

An appropriate method of demolition is cited against each item.

Citizen Commodities and Responsibilities:

In his private capacity as well as in trade, business, industry or administration, the plain citizen owns things which the enemy must not get hold of:

Such are:

Survey and scientific instruments, binoculars, cameras &c.

Maps, even ordinary tourist and advertising maps.

Radio receiving sets - especially battery sets.

Tools - axes, mattocks, shovels, picks, etc.

Rope, tennis nets, string and twine - these can be used for camouflage nets.

Water - tanks and drums.

Oil tanks, drums and tins.

Firearms and ammunition.

Explosives.

Launches and small craft.

Petrol, diesel fuels, oils, greases, kerosene.

Power alcohols, charcoal.

Tyres, rubber hoses, &c.

Trucks, lorries, cycles, cars, buses, trailers.

Horses, and saddles and harness.

Waggons, drays, sulkies, buggies.

Boots, sandshoes, blankets and sheets, cotton
     and woollen goods, and clothing and leather.

Motor tools and accessories.

Batteries.

Tents.

Foodstuffs.

Spirits, liquors, beers, are of special
     importance. Cattle, sheep, pigs, poultry.

Grain and seed.

Haystacks, ensilage, growing crops.

Pastoral and farming machinery, implements and
     equipment.

First aid and medical supplies and soap.

The ordinary citizen may be called upon to destroy for his country's sake rather than yield them to the enemy, possessions which to him were treasured.

This sacrifice will be demanded of him as a civil soldier lest the enemy acquire these things to use them against us for our own destruction.

But only at the last moment when enemy pressure is such that we may be forced to leave a sector of our country in occupation, and open to rapine and pillage.

In any case the enemy will never give up what has come into his hands, for he will finally destroy when we force his withdrawal, or as with the bronze doors from the banks of Singapore, remove them to Japan, or as with the machinery at Hongkong, ship them to Manchukuo,[2] or as with the rubber in Malaya, start shipment with his first toehold.

Over the potential battlefields, the civil utilities, properties, stores and materials to be denied to the enemy, are vast and widespread.

The Fighting Forces and their Engineer and Salvage Troops will be busy enough in front line duties.

We do not know where the enemy will choose to strike, or what point he will reach.

Plain citizens must, therefore, lend a hand - <u>everywhere</u>!

<u>The Citizen's Role:</u>

In traditional warfare the citizen was a neutral, non-combatant.

The populace pursued its peacetime avocations - whilst uniformed armies fought according to rules and textbooks. The Mayor, in his robes of office, handed over to the conqueror the keys of the city.

In Total War -

ø/ The enemy uses disguise, fifth columnism,[3] paratrooping, infiltration, treachery.

ø/ The citizenry is bombed, machine gunned, air-raided, incendiarised, terrorised -

ø/ And is stampeded against its own defending forces in order to screen the enemy advance, to obstruct the defending army, to produce panic, demoralisation, defeatism.

ø/ The population in occupied territories is reduced to unfed slavery; its women are raped, its children wantonly killed or maimed -

ø/ The enemy strips the country of valuable materials, plant, machinery; and transfers them for his own enrichment.

ø/ <u>Leaving, a Scorched Earth behind him, in which civilians fend for themselves in the</u>

ruins, and are left to implore their country's
allies, as in Greece, for "wheat or coffins".

This is Modern War - as taught and practised by
Germany and Japan.

The Australian answer to Total War must be, as in
Russia and China, total citizen collaboration with
the armed forces.

The citizen may be still non-combatant - because
he hasn't a rifle - <u>but</u> he is <u>not</u> neutral.

<u>Every Australian is required to collaborate in
Scorched Earth operations.</u>

If he doesn't, the fighting forces will have to
do this additional job for him, when they might be
better occupied killing Japanese.

Scorched Earth Organisation is the job of the
Civil Arm.

But the civil soldier will wait for the military
order or until the enemy is in sight - before he does
the job and makes his getaway.

When the Australian knows his action station, no
Japanese can shift him from it till he is finished.

Whether he wears the uniform or not makes no
difference to his Australian spirit.

Our most tragic shortage is the shortage of time,
however.

Every citizen must get busy <u>now</u>.

That is his first war duty -

Instantly to organise for Scorched Earth
operations and to successfully implement them at
last moments.

<u>Scorched Earth Support Squads as Citizen Aids:</u>

Last moment citizen actions near the front line
are liable to accidents, confusion, and misfiring.

Therefore special Scorched Earth Support Squads
will be organised in each centre.

The jobs of Support Squads will be:

(i)   <u>In the first place</u> to help citizens in prompt
        and careful planning of their arrangements
        to ensure last moment denial of their
        possessions to the enemy.

(ii)   <u>In the last place</u>, to reinforce and support
        citizens in last moment demolitions and to
        see that <u>no</u> plan misfires.

Any member of a Support Squad, or of the Military,
or of the Police Forces is authorised to enforce
instructions and to complete them at owner's cost,
if not completed in an effective or timely way.

Co-operation, however, is what is called for from
every Australian.

Citizens should welcome and work with the Support
Squads against the Japanese - and be more ruthless
than the enemy.

Our combined job is to beat him at Total War - and
live to build again.

War Damage and Scorched Earth Insurance:

The British Colonial Code provides, in respect of
compensation for war damages:

"Where damage is done in the course of military
operations, or on orders of our own Forces, the
answer to any enquiries must be that the question
of compensation cannot be decided until after the
completion of the war."

Australia has enacted the War Damage Insurance
Act which covers loss through Scorched Earth
operations.

Every citizen may and should insure his
possessions against war damage and scorched earth
operations under this War Damages Insurance Act.

This Act pools and shares the civil losses of war;
if not availed of, the neglecting citizen must carry
his own loss himself.

NATIONAL SECURITY (Scorched Earth) Regulations - Military Powers:

"Scorched earth" is a military operation under
military control. The plain citizen, whether in his
home or in his job, is required immediately to make
ready for instant demolition at military signal and
command, all things which are to be denied to the
enemy.

Every citizen will be held responsible, in
respect of the things in his possession or control,
for denying them to the enemy, at all hazard to
himself.

This is a citizen's action station and battle order.

National Security Regulations have been
approved - called Scorched Earth Regulations - which
give all necessary powers to the Army, and which
require the civilian to carry out the war duties
sketched above.

Dispersal and Disposal First:

After military operations are deemed by the Army
to have commenced:

(i)   The civilian population must "stay put" - so
        as not to impede the operations of its own
        fighting forces by enemy-created stampedes,
        and refugee road congestions.
(ii)   No civilian evacuation of any kind,
        from either town or country, can then be
        permitted - except under direct military
        orders and control.
(iii)   The military may permit late evacuation from
        country sectors via non-military roads,

of essential motor vehicles transferring
essential wartime materials - or carrying
only women, girls, boys under 16, or aged
infirm males, with priority to relatives of
citizens engaged near the front line in the
more hazardous citizen collaboration duties.

(iv)   Otherwise able-bodied males stay on the job,
carrying on in Labor Corps, Scorched Earth
and other approved citizen collaboration
actions.

There is no sense in leaving for last moment
destruction anything that can be prior dispersed or
disposed of.

After military action begins, dispersal is too
late; and the resulting salvage too little!

What can be done should be done beforehand.

That means NOW!

It is again the citizen's job.

ø/ Civil development must be suspended until we
win - to build a New Age!

ø/ Warlike and wartime essential production
must be accelerated though battles rage - and
be continued to the last moment.

ø/ Hoarding must cease; supplies must be kept
low by dispersal of concentrations.

ø/ There must be similar dispersal of young
stock, cattle, sheep &c. - seed, valuable
plant, machinery, essential vehicles, spare
parts, materials and supplies generally.

ø/ Tools, food and supply caches should be
located and established in the bush.

ø/ Rather than keep them in disuse until they
have finally to be destroyed, the citizen
should hand over to the Military authorities
at once, things which the Army urgently
needs, e.g.:

Survey and scientific instruments,
binoculars and cameras.

Maps.

Battery radio sets.

Rope.

Firearms and ammunition.

Explosives.

Tyres.

Trucks, cars, cycles, bicycles, tractors.

Tools.

Tents.

ø/ Civilians and civil industry should plan for
final last-moment local dispersal, or disposal
or salvage of irreplaceable things by:

  (i)   Prior location of hiding places, or
         digging of holes or trenches, in which
         quickly moveable things - e.g. tools,
         foodstuffs - can be hurriedly buried
         or hidden beyond reach of the enemy at
         last moment.

  (ii)   Prior sorting out of things into items
         (i) for transfer to the Army; (ii) for
         hurried hiding or burying; (iii) for
         dispersal among the people likely to be
         left under Japanese occupation; (iv) to
         be denied to the invader by last-moment
         destruction.

The citizen must work out as applicable to his
own case and his own possessions, the most effective
means of putting out of reach or out of action what
he might otherwise have to yield to the enemy in a
military emergency.

DESTRUCTION - Simple, Silent, Selective, Swift!

The Scorched Earth war-job must not be imagined to
be a riotous, excited, noisy, loose, destruction of
everything in sight.

Nor have we to encourage the enemy and depress our own fighting men, by noisily beating for a week beforehand, the drums of retreat; and publishing smoke and flame and detonations in our rear, in unworthy anticipation of enemy victory.

Scorched Earth is a disciplined, selective, aggressive operation; depending upon thorough preparation beforehand; <u>for unmiserly consummation against the enemy at the final military moment!</u>

It needs to be carried through as simply, as silently, as secretly, as swiftly as possible!

It needs to be complete enough to utterly deny our resources to the enemy.

If we do have to use fire and explosives, we should try to involve the enemy in both!

But do not start off with the preconceived notion that large quantities of explosives, fuses, detonators, primer cord and so on are necessary to destroy the articles and stocks in our ordinary possession.

Only large plants, bridges, and undertakings in the installation and public utility class call for such methods. And even many of these can be rendered immediately useless by their expert staffs who know the vital and irreplaceable parts, and how to smash them with an axe or sledge hammer, or otherwise.

Nor is fire the universal destructant.

Many things will not burn. And even in the cases of those which will burn, the fires ignited may go out before the destruction is complete.

So if you burn – smash before you burn; and be sure to smash the vital, irreplaceable parts.

But you may also hide, bury, submerge, wet, scatter, contaminate, or take bush!

There is an appropriate best method for every type of installation and material. The experts of

the industry are the best advisers on this, and they
have been consulted before drafting the recommended
method of destruction for each item of the Scorched
Earth Category.

Have everything ready - everywhere!

Let everyone help!

War is Hell!

But we are in it!

Collaborate with the A.M.F.

THE SCORCHED EARTH CODE ITSELF:

This Scorched Earth Code has been prepared by
the State War Effort Co-Ordination Committee, as
a directional guide to citizens, to industries and
services, in the:

(i)   Framing of Action details for their local
        unit operations.

(ii)   Immediate completion of prior arrangements
        for swift and timely consummation at military
        signal - or on the too close approach of the
        enemy.

        The Code has two sections:
        1. General - Citizen Code (for citizens
           primarily).
        2. Specialised - Industrial and Services'
           Code.

The first section deals with things in the
possession or use of the ordinary citizen-at-home,
or widespread over the civil structure, so that the
private citizen as such is primarily responsible for
them.

The second deals with special businesses, trades,
industries and administrations, for which the
organisations are managerially responsible. It
consists of separates for each, and has no further
place in this publication.

(<u>Note</u>: (i) Every user-in-possession will be
              responsible to the Scorched Earth
              National Security Regulations, at all
              hazards to himself, for the <u>denial to</u>
              <u>the enemy</u> of what he is using or what he
              possesses.

                     Such denial shall take the form,
                     either of:
                     (a) Destruction beyond hope of
                         repair.
                     (b) Hiding, burying, submerging,
                         prior dispersal or disposal –
                         beyond possible discovery by the
                         enemy: salvaging – e.g. tyres,
                         batteries, and irreplaceable
                         parts if possible – and so on:
              and will be implemented at military
              signal or on too close approach of
              the enemy and prior to abandonment).

(<u>Note (ii)</u> Every employer, manager, or supervisor,
              will be equally responsible;
              (a) For the fulfilment of denial by his
                  employees or subordinates.
              (b) For prior drafting of Action details
                  for his unit organisation.
              (c) For prior preparation, arrangement,
                  and staff exercises, to assure
                  effective last-moment fulfilment).

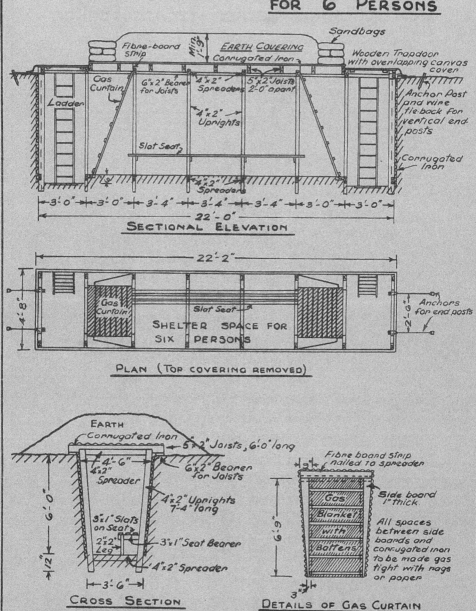

GARDEN TRENCH AIR RAID SHELTER
FOR 6 PERSONS

Sectional Elevation labels: Fibre-board strip · Min. 1'-9" · EARTH COVERING · Corrugated Iron · Sandbags · Wooden Trapdoor with overlapping canvas cover · Gas Curtain · 6"x2" Bearer for Joists · 4"x2" Spreaders · 5"x2" Joists 2'-0" apart · 4"x2" Uprights · Ladder · Slat Seat · 4"x2" Spreaders · Anchor Post and wire tie-back for vertical end posts · Corrugated Iron

Dimensions: 3'-0" · 3'-0" · 3'-4" · 3'-4" · 3'-4" · 3'-0" · 3'-0" · 22'-0"

SECTIONAL ELEVATION

Plan labels: 22'-2" · 4'-8" · Gas Curtain · Slat Seat · 2'-6" · Anchors for end posts · SHELTER SPACE FOR SIX PERSONS

PLAN (TOP COVERING REMOVED)

Cross Section labels: Earth · Corrugated Iron · 5"x2" Joists, 6'-0" long · 4'-6" · 4"x2" Spreader · 6"x2" Bearer for Joists · 4"x2" Uprights 7'-4" long · 3"x1" Slats on Seat · 2"x2" Leg · 3"x1" Seat Bearer · 4"x2" Spreader · 6'-0" · 1/2" · 3'-6"

CROSS SECTION

Details of Gas Curtain labels: Fibre board strip nailed to spreader · Gas Blanket with Battens · Side board 1" thick · All spaces between side boards and corrugated iron to be made gas tight with rags or paper · 6'-9" · 3"

DETAILS OF GAS CURTAIN

3

THE GENERAL
CITIZEN CODE

After outlining the basic aims of the Code, the subcommittee—
sounding very much like Swain in his initial trumpet call
(Chapter 1)—explained what it meant for ordinary citizens. Noting
the many items in ordinary homes and garages that were of potential
value to an invasion force, it urged people to act immediately. If
they could not hide or disperse them, they should make plans for
destroying them at short notice.

All forms of private transport, from rowboats to cars, bicycles
and horse-drawn wagons should be assessed. Those that were not
essential—or which could not be used because of petrol rationing—
should be sent inland, buried, sunk or smashed. Boats and motor
vehicles were so important that they had their own section of the
Code (reproduced in Chapters 6 and 8).

If an invasion took place and evacuation became necessary,
householders were to destroy or dump all food, and take special
care to leave no alcohol behind. In preparation for evacuation,
they were to set aside a week's rations, providing for each adult: '¼
lb tea; ½ lb sugar; 1 lb slab of chocolate; 1 tin of condensed milk;
3 x 8 oz tins beef; 2 lbs rice; Bovril'.

Houses and furniture could remain intact, but cooking utensils, light bulbs, refrigerator and vacuum cleaner motors, radio valves and telephones were on the destruction list. Clothing (including tennis shoes, 'the Jap's favourite'), blankets, maps and binoculars were also to be burned, smashed or buried—as were any tools not wanted by the Army. Guttering and water tanks were to be punctured, and horses and livestock not already requisitioned by the Army or moved inland were to be slaughtered.

Workers were urged to take the initiative and assume 'personal responsibility' for finding the most efficient and cost-effective ways 'to deny to the Japanese invader what he depends upon for our conquest!'

GENERAL CITIZEN CODE

1. <u>BOATS AND WATERCRAFT.</u>

   <u>Military reason</u>: The Japanese are born watermen
   and boatmen; and in their warfare have sweepingly
   requisitioned craft for coastwise penetrations
   and river outflankings and infiltrations.
   A waiting boat is an invasion hazard!

   Watercraft consist of:

   (i) Pleasure and non-essential craft.

   (ii) Economic or commercial craft.

   The first are being towed for the Navy to
   concentrated moorings where the Army will take
   over responsibility, remove engines and salvage
   vital parts: the State War Effort Co-ordination
   Committee Scorched Earth auxiliaries are handling
   the job for both Arms, and will be responsible for
   maintenance, guard, and emergency demolition.

   <u>The second group as yet remain available for
   either commercial or enemy use!</u>

   In Malaya, fish are a staple article of native
   diet, and fishing an essential industry of first
   importance.

   Yet the A.I.F., after first bitter experience
   of Japanese requisitioning, had no further
   compunction in destroying the fishing boats and
   the Malayan fishing industry!

   As a first provision for Total War in
   Australia, we may have to dispense with seafoods,
   to deny both them and watercraft to an enemy to
   whom both are vital.

   We can eat mutton: the Japanese dislike it!

   Until <u>all</u> boats are removed from our coastal,
   and estuarine waters, every citizen owner or user
   in effect points a loaded gun against us.

   Be watchful of that "gun"!

Do not leave a boat unguarded, without removing
petrol, rudder, rowlocks, oars, and vital parts.

Moor it in hiding.

Pass it over to the Scorched Earth crows before
compulsion becomes urgent. Or beach it on the
spring tide and dismantle it and camouflage it.

Do not leave port without advising the
Fisheries Inspector, or the Police, of your
course or return.

Be watchful for the enemy! Scuttle your boat to
deny it to him.

2. MOTOR AND OTHER VEHICLES.
(Including trailers, bicycles, tractors, wagons,
drays, sulkies, buggies, horses &c.)

Military reason: The Japanese did not bring many
motor vehicles to Malaya - they depended on local
requisitioning - and succeeded! The Australians
learned to smash Malayan bicycles viciously -
they had cost them dear! Deny the enemy your
vehicles, and you clip his advance!

Apart from the military reason, invasion
would dislocate our railways which are already
overloaded. Our entire motor fleet would be badly
needed for our own use.

If we have the petrol!

What vehicles we cannot use, we must dismantle
or dispose of at once!

What we have to abandon in crisis, we must
first destroy!

Every non-motor vehicle must be put to work!

Unsold or unregistered motor vehicles:
dispersal or dismantling.

With military approval, the motor trade
will be allotted sufficient petrol to disperse
concentration of unsold vehicles to country
centres more than 50 miles from the coast.

Owners of unregistered vehicles may be given
the same facilities.

In either case the petrol allowed will be
sufficient only to transfer the vehicles once and
for all to approved places.

When such transfers take place, the
vehicles should be used also to disperse trade
concentrations of tyres and spare parts, radio
sets, petrol, lubricating oils &c. - subject
always to the "freezing" regulations. Every
vehicle should be fully loaded.

All vehicles suitable for military purposes
should be offered to the military authorities -
now!

Unregistered vehicles which have been
"jacked up" for the duration of the war should
be dismantled now - disposing of spare wheels,
tyres, batteries, distributors, tools and spare
parts to registered owners or traders.

Or, if of a type suitable for military
purposes, dismantling and labelling parts with
owner's name and address, and vehicle type - ready
to transfer to military, N.E.S., or other use on
demand.

(Note: As imports of petrol, vehicles, and spare
        parts for civilian use have ceased for
        the duration of the war, and there will
        be shortage for military and economic
        purposes, it is obviously both economic
        and patriotic for owners of unused
        vehicles so to proceed: or else to convert
        to producer gas for vehicle use in
        essential services.)

Or effectively burying or hiding the parts
beyond possibility of enemy discovery.

Or finally destroying the whole vehicle.

There will be no last minute evacuation of
any but absolutely essential vehicles - and no
vehicle must remain within reach of the enemy in a
useable condition.

<u>Registered Vehicles:</u>

All registered motor vehicles must be
effectively serviced every evening, with petrol
or charcoal at the full, in readiness for
emergency.

Late evacuations of <u>essential</u> registered motor
vehicles may be permitted in country districts by
the military via non-military roads, subject to
their transferring essential warlike or wartime
stores and/or women, girls, boys under 16, or aged
infirm.

Late evacuations from the cities, if permitted,
will be by public transport supplemented by
private vehicles pressed into service by the
responsible authority.

All vehicles must be destroyed before
abandonment. This applies also to assembled motor
vehicles in dealers' or distributors' stocks.

Drivers or users must make themselves
acquainted beforehand with the given methods of
destruction.

Outside the city of Sydney, each must carry an
axe, suitable tools, and a bottle of inflammable
liquid.

<u>Salvage and Destruction before Abandonment:</u>

Before abandoning, the vehicle must be driven
off the road out of the way - unless directed by
a military officer to form part of a military
obstruction.

If possible, prior to abandonment, the
driver must salvage spare wheels, tyres, tools,
batteries, spare parts, and transfer them to late
evacuation trains or motor vehicles.

Otherwise, he must irrevocably immobilise or destroy the vehicle in the manner hereunder:

(Note: Denial of similar parts of every car
        is essential as the basic plan. This is
        to prevent the repair of some vehicles
        by collecting parts from others. The
        distributor must be removed from every car
        whatever other steps are taken to complete
        denial).

(1) <u>Motor Vehicles without Petrol</u>:
     Remove and destroy distributor housing
     complete.
     Remove wheels, starting with spare - or slash
        or saw through tyres.
     Remove batteries, or smash with axe or
        hammer.
     Smash cylinder head.
     Break bottle of inflammable liquid or heap
        inflammable material over car; and ignite.
     If removed parts and tools cannot be salvaged
        and transferred, hide, bury, smash and/or
        throw into the burning vehicles. If buried
        in safety, wrap in oily rag and place in a
        container if time permits.

(2) <u>Motor Vehicles with Petrol</u>:
     Puncture radiator and sump.
     Start engine and leave running at full speed,
        to seize engine.
     Slash or saw tyres, and smash petrol tank and
        distributor after engine seizes.
     Splash petrol inside the vehicle and ignite.

(3) <u>Motor Vehicles on Producer Gas</u>:
     If the producer is alight act as in (2)
        above.
     If producer is cold act as in (1) and in
        addition smash mixing valve and hopper.

What to do in an air raid

USE BUCKETS of sand, shovel, and hoe to deal with incendiary bomb. Do not approach till splutter subsides.

TURN KITCHEN UTENSILS upside down so that glass splinters or powdered glass from shattered windows or fanlights will not get into them. Powdered glass fatalities occurred in England.

STICKING PAPER or adhesive tape across windows in lattice design will prevent glass from shattering. Use any type of paper.

TIP SAND onto floor, leaving some in bucket. Hold hoe and shovel together to save time. Cover bomb with sand.

IF CAUGHT at distance from shelter lie in the gutter, raising chest, stomach and lower part of body by resting on arms. Keep mouth open and cover the head as much as possible, using hat or coat.

KEEP AN EYEBATH in the bathroom to bathe the eyes should there be persistent gas contamination. Use warm saline solution.

COVER SHOVEL with sand, then rake bomb onto it. Do not let bomb touch naked metal as it will burn through.

HALLWAYS are recommended for shelter and a table is good protection against falling plaster, glass and debris. Make yourself comfortable with a cushion and rug. Listen to the radio or read a book.

TIP BOMB into bucket, partially filled with sand. Cover with sand and carry into the garden.

HOUSEHOLDERS are also recommended to smother bombs with bags of sand. Make them something like these, used by Fire Brigades. Crouch low, as heat rises.

THIS SHOWS how to drop bag over incendiary. Bag should be dropped over top of bomb, not thrown. This should not be done if bomb is burning too fiercely.

(4) <u>Trailers:</u>

Smash spokes.

Smash axle (including differential if any,
   and springs).

Burn if possible.

(5) <u>Tractors:</u>

Tractors are indispensable for military
   works and are urgently required.

If not fully engaged on essential wartime
production, they should be made available to
the Army <u>now</u> - or dispersed from the coastal
areas.

On no account must they be allowed to fall
into enemy hands.

Destruction on approach of the enemy must
be carried out - by one or other of the
following methods:

(a) Drain sump and radiator, start the
     engine at full speed - then:
     Puncture fuel tank, and ignite.

or:

(b) Remove the distributor housing complete
     and destroy - or wrap in an oil rag,
     place in a container and bury or hide in
     a place known only to the user and not
     discoverable by the enemy.

or:

(c) Drop a stick of gelignite into the sump
     and ignite.

or:

(d) Run over a cliff.

If not on essential work, tractors should be
evacuated from coastal areas or handed over
to the Military NOW.

(6) <u>Motor tools and accessories:</u>

Break, smash, cut, burn or otherwise destroy

or throw into deep water (sea, river or
lake) or bury in a well concealed place.
Smashing of electrical equipment especially
distributors, is particularly important.
Batteries - smash with an axe.

(7) Bicycles:

Bicycles were freely requisitioned by the
Japanese in Malaya.
They must not fall into their hands in
Australia.
The user will be individually responsible
for denying bicycles to the enemy.
Destruction methods are:

    Bend or break forks.
    Slash the tyres beyond repair.
    Slash the wheel spokes beyond repair.
    Remove chain, handlebars and tools and
    bury or hide beyond discovery - or throw
    into deep water.

(8) Wagons, drays, sulkies and buggies - and
horses:

In the likelihood of cessation of petrol
imports, these older means of conveyance
acquire importance. They should be used for
early evacuations or transfers of women,
children, and essential goods -
Or hidden in the bush.
In the last resort they must be denied to the
enemy: thus
Vehicles:
Smash spokes of all wheels and shafts.
Burn.
Remove or bury chains and other essentials.
Animals:
Any horses that cannot be evacuated before
military operations commence must be

destroyed if there be danger of their falling
into enemy hands.

All fodder must be burned or otherwise
destroyed.

All harness that cannot be removed must be
buried or destroyed by fire or slashing.

3. FOODSTUFFS, CLOTHING, AND HOUSEHOLD EFFECTS.

Military reason: Events in the Pacific war so far
have shown that the enemy has been greatly helped
by his ability to live on the country and thus
reduce his transport of stores, both by sea and
by land. So he must be forced as far as is humanly
possible, to bring his own food and clothing with
him and thus make himself more vulnerable.

(i) Foodstuffs:

Every kind of foodstuff will be of use
to the enemy, and denial will have to be
particularly complete in view of his ability
to live on what would be very short rations
for an Australian.

The Asiatic worker is normally able to live
on a diet which may not extend beyond rice,
green vegetables and a very little fish or
canned meat.

SALT IS VITAL TO HIM AND NONE MUST BE LEFT
FOR HIM!

Bulk Stores: These are dealt with more
particularly under the Industrial and
Services Code which covers the complete
denial of perishable and non-perishable
stocks.

Wholesalers and retailers of foodstuffs:

(a) will maintain their stocks at minimum
     levels;

(b) will see to it that, when occupation
     of a district by the enemy becomes

imminent, stocks are as far as possible
distributed to the public in quantities
which they can reasonably use and which
they can easily destroy in the last
extremity.

(In this connexion, plans should be made NOW
to cache foodstuffs in places where they will
not easily be found by the enemy but where
they will be available to the citizen who
has to "stay put". Hiding places should be
planned at once, and holes or trenches dug in
suitable and convenient places so that food
may be hidden at a moment's notice.
What foods will be put in these caches must
be decided NOW and the means of protecting
non-tinned foods devised. Only the most
nutritious and least perishable types
(particularly tinned foods including milk)
should be set aside for hiding. The rest will
be dispersed as above or destroyed.)
Householders are expected to refrain
entirely from hoarding, but they should set
aside, against war's emergency, a week's
supply of absolute essentials which could be
easily hidden or carried, if necessary.

These essentials need not exceed for one
adult:-
¼ lb. tea; ½ lb. sugar; 1 lb. slab chocolate;
1 tin condensed milk; 3 x 8 oz. tins beef;
2 lbs. rice; Bovril (plus simple first-aid
remedies)or something similar.

All other foodstuffs, if they cannot be
disposed of otherwise, must be destroyed or
thoroughly adulterated. The householder will
easily devise ways and means of making food
useless for human consumption by adulteration
with kerosene or disinfectants; by mixing

sand with sugar; by scattering powdered
foodstuffs such as flour and other cereals,
sugar, salt on the ground; and, of course, by
dumping in rivers, lakes or the sea.

Non-perishable and easily transportable
foodstuffs such as those packed in tins must
be given special attention since their value
is enhanced by their keeping qualities.
If you cannot cache them beyond hope of
discovery by the enemy, smash all tins at
the very least and if possible destroy or
adulterate the contents as well.

<u>No brandy or other spirits, or beers or
wines must be left for the enemy</u>. This is
vital. Smash the bottles. There is abundance
of spirits elsewhere for our use.

(ii) <u>Clothing</u>:

In the pleasant climate of N.S.W., clothing
is much less important to the Japanese than
it is to the Germans in Russia.

But, at the same time, campaigning must not
be made easier for the enemy by leaving him
any useful garments.

The Japanese does not recognise any rules
of war, and disguise has been very useful to
him so far. So do not leave any clothes that
will help to protect him from recognition by
our troops until it is too late.

Clothes should be destroyed by cutting
or by fire. Boots should be slashed, but in
particular sox; and the Jap's. favourite
tennis shoes must be destroyed.

Leave no blankets.

(iii) <u>Household effects</u>:

It is not intended that the scorched earth
should be extended to the destruction of

houses or furniture, neither of which will be
particularly helpful.
But -
Leave no cooking utensils and in particular
  hide or dump in deep water all aluminium
  utensils.
Smash electric bulbs.
Smash motors of vacuum cleaners.
Smash refrigerator generators
  and
Don't forget to dispose of or destroy all
maps, cameras, and field glasses.
Tools: Hand over to the Army all tools - saws,
axes, shovels, hammers, chisels and others
that could be put to use by the enemy - or
hide in prior prepared holes or in the bush,
or dump in deep water. Be ready for emergency.
Wireless sets and telephones: Make wireless
sets useless by removing and hiding or by
destroying valves and other important parts
such as transformers.
But, better still, smash completely.
(Note:- Battery sets that can be saved and
            handed over to the Army should be
            so handed over. They could prove
            invaluable for communication
            purposes in the field.)
Smash telephone instruments beyond
recognition and cut leads to your own
house. The Japanese use the telephone for
communications.
(Note:- Don't interfere with main telephone
            lines. You may cause havoc by cutting
            an important line of communication.
            These lines will be dealt with by the
            Army or P.M.G.)

<u>4</u>. <u>DOMESTIC WATER SUPPLIES.</u>

The denial of water may in many places in
Australia be quite as important as the more
spectacular denial of oil and petrol.

The denial of water in reticulation systems
will be the duty of the water authorities, but
the householder who gets his supplies from
wells by bucket, pump, or windmill or from roof
catchments discharging into tanks, must accept
responsibility for his own arrangements.

Therefore, upon emergency withdrawal, destroy
the means of collecting or storing water in farm
or home.

Destroy guttering and downpipes.

Puncture tanks.

Destroy head-gear of wells.

Pollute well water.

Destroy all pumps.

Destroy windmills or other machinery operating
water pumps.

Smash as much piping as possible.

<u>5</u>. <u>STOCK, FODDER, CROPS, FARM MACHINERY.</u>

<u>Prior dispersal of stock:</u> Arrangements have
already been made and carried out for dispersal of
young stock to inland areas. These arrangements
naturally include all necessary provisions for
food and water.

(i) <u>Stock:</u>

Such stock as may be left in vulnerable areas
must not be allowed to fall into the hands of
the enemy. Beasts remaining in paddocks will
have to be slaughtered if abandonment should
become militarily necessary. If the meat
can be distributed to military or civilians,
this must be done, but otherwise all possible

steps must be taken to render it unfit for
human consumption. Plan NOW.

Horses will have been put into service with
the Army or civilian auxiliaries but any
that might fall into enemy hands must be
destroyed. Their harness must also be made
useless by slashing or burning. This may
seem unnecessary after the horse is dead
but destruction of all horses may not be
complete.

(ii) Fodder, crops, grain and seed:

Every farmer will plan NOW so that he can
destroy all haystacks, cereal stocks and
other feed that might have to be abandoned
in emergency. The destruction, if and when
commanded, must be complete.

He should therefore devise plans NOW which
will enable him to deny to the enemy to
the greatest extent that circumstances and
season will permit, all kinds of food and
fodder crops that may be in the field.

(iii) Farm machinery:

There must be complete denial to the enemy
of all tractors and internal combustion or
electric power units. Denial methods for
the former will be found in Section 2 of
the General Citizen Code. Electric motors
and generators can be put out of action by
smashing the casing.

Destroy switchboards.

Destroy batteries.

Destroy lamps.

Smash chaff-cutters, and mills.

Remove and hide ploughs, harrows and any
other implements that are difficult to
destroy.

Remove cutting parts of reapers and
harvesters and bury them.
Add don't forget the denial of water as set
out in Section 3.

Poster for Civil Construction Corps, 1942.

THE CITIZEN-IN-INDUSTRY:

A special Scorched Earth Industrial Code is
being issued to the managements of Industrial and
Manufacturing plants and to bodies controlling
Public Utility Services.

The plain citizen will find himself, in many
cases, absorbed into these special schemes, but
it is important that he should realise to the full
that he has a personal as well as a general duty, to
see that any scorched earth plan, to which he may
be detailed in connexion with his job, is properly
understood and will be properly carried out.

Some of the plans call for the use of explosives
in demolition, but the job may have to be done
without explosives in certain circumstances - for
example, they may not be available or they may fail
to do the damage expected - and to guard against any
eventuality the citizen himself should decide what
he could do with simple means (say, with a sledge
hammer) to make a real good job.

Small industries, repair shops and the like:
In small concerns the whole responsibility for
denial of machines and materials will fall upon
the man on the spot, and he can expect advice but
must not depend for assistance upon scorched earth
organisations. The Government relies on managers
and workers to see that their plans are complete and
their determination firm to carry them out at the
word of command.

Special industries and services:

For the purpose of Scorched Earth planning, the
following categories have been accepted:-

Industry.	Utility Services.
Craft - sail and power.	Bulk wool.
Industrial stocks and raw materials.	" flour.
	" grain.
" power.	Coal Mines.
" water supply and manufacturing plant & machinery.	Communication and transport systems.
	Electricity, gas.
Machine shops & repair equipment.	Landings and jetties.
	Road-making plant.
Motor fuels - storage.	Water supply.
" transport.	

It may be stated broadly that there is no article
or commodity made or grown in this country or
imported to it that would not fit into some part of
the enemy's war-machine or economy.

If the enemy should effect a landing in Australia,
there is nothing more certain than that the
transports that brought his troops and materials,
will go back to their bases, in the Islands or in
Japan, loaded with whatever machinery, plant, goods
or raw materials are surplus to his local needs!

Apart from materials, he would be greatly aided
in maintaining a footing if he could bring and take
to his own use, our machines and power, could extend
his communications and improvise his defence works
with our equipment and maintain his whole structure
on the power of our oil, our coal, our electricity
and our gas.

We must see to it, therefore, that no useful
manufactures, raw materials, machinery or sources
of power fall into the enemy's hands intact.

Destruction must be sufficiently selective to
ensure that all the things most important to the

enemy are dealt with whatever happens, and the
methods must be sufficiently thorough to ensure
complete denial.

This does not mean that the aim should be less
than the total denial of everything but simply that
if time and circumstances limit the action possible,
then the most important things should be dealt with
first.

In every case the aim should be the most thorough
destruction by the simplest methods.

· If a sledge hammer will demolish a machine, why
use explosives which might be used to make a land-
mine?

The suggestions made in regard to each category
are only suggestions - they are good ways of
carrying out the job, but if you can think of a
better one, by all means use it.

The enemy will be more effectively hampered if the
same item of machinery or the corresponding vital
part of a particular type of machine or installation
is denied in every case than if one item or part is
destroyed in one place and a different one in another.

Special attention should therefore be paid to the
destruction of independent prime-movers and steam-
boilers, so that no source of power for any purpose
may be available.

The resulting scrap-iron, much desired by the
Japanese, leaves a final problem; to be solved by
the exercise of our every possible means and device.

FINALLY:
Scorched Earth plans for special services and
industries have been drafted in consultation with
these services and industries, and are available
to unit managements as guides in the preparation of
their own Action Details -

<u>to deny to the Japanese invader what he depends upon</u>
<u>for our conquest!</u>

    THE PRODUCTS OF OUR HANDS AND LANDS!

ø/ Thus may we help to keep Australia a free
    democracy!

            GOD SAVE THE KING!

—————————

4

THE GENERAL INDUSTRY CODE

The owners and managers of farms, factories and mills were directly addressed in the second part of the Scorched Earth Code. They were urged to immediately make detailed plans so that they would be ready to implement the denial policy as soon as the Army issued the order. By then the enemy would be closing in and there would be no time to waste. Business owners were warned that the Japanese would try to seize lightly defended areas before 'converging . . . on the fortified industrial zones'. Those in coastal areas outside the Newcastle-Sydney-Port Kembla strip were to start preparing at once.

All factories and businesses were asked to list their machines and equipment, stocks of raw materials and finished products; detail how these would be wrecked, buried or disabled; and name the individuals appointed to carry out the denial tasks. These lists were to be submitted to the Army for approval. Businesses that contributed to the War Damages Fund would receive compensation if their property had to be destroyed to deny it to the enemy.

The subcommittee tried to cover every type of trade and business, from garages to tanneries to soap factories. It gave broad instructions for disabling a huge variety of tools and equipment, including drills, power units, compressors, forges, vehicle jacks, optical lenses, batteries, mills, chemical vats, looms, slipways, distilleries, canning machinery, saws, cranes, tent making equipment, rubber vulcanising machinery, cameras and film. In the case of engines and machinery too large to destroy completely at short notice, vital parts were to be identified for removal or destruction. The aim in every case was 'the most thorough destruction by the simplest methods'.

DENIAL OF RESOURCES TO THE ENEMY
N.S.W. L. OF C. AREA.[1]

CIRCULAR TO INDUSTRIES: DENIAL OF MACHINERY,
EQUIPMENT, PLANT, AND STOCKS, IN FACTORIES,
WORKSHOPS, WAREHOUSES AND STORES &C.

At Army request the State War Effort Co-ordination Committee is endeavouring to cover every civil eventuality of war, and through its Scorched Earth Sub-Committee is investigating and planning for the completest possible denial to the enemy of all local aids to war, should he secure foothold in Australia.

This policy of denial is called "Scorched Earth", although normally, the denial will be selective rather than devastative.

In the contingency of actual invasion and occupation of any sector, the need for such denial to the enemy of all our resources of transport, power, machinery and raw materials will be apparent to you if you recall the extent to which the Axis powers have harnessed to their war-machine the industrial resources of Europe, and if you consider how much more vulnerable will be the Japanese transport lines if all his supplies have to be brought by sea and not secured from the country invaded.

For these reasons there can be no doubt that should the need arise you will not require the Government to invoke powers of compulsion in applying a Scorched Earth plan, but, realising its importance to Australia and the United Nations,[2] you will give with willingness the fullest instant co-operation, and will collaborate in that degree of preparation which alone can make Scorched Earth an effective weapon with which to strike the enemy.

If actual implementation becomes necessary, the Army will give the order and you will be expected, as a responsible management and citizen, to put into action plans which you will already have formulated on the general lines of the hints which follow.

The denial command will be issued by the Army only if danger is imminent and enemy pressure critical. In such case little time will remain for the implementation of the prepared action detail and the selected staff must hold themselves in readiness to receive the Army order from the Zone Control Officer.

Destruction must be sufficiently selective to ensure that all the things most important to the enemy are dealt with whatever happens, and the methods must be sufficiently thorough to ensure complete denial for as long as possible.

This does not mean that the aim should be less than the total denial of everything, but simply that, if time and circumstances limit the action possible, then the most important things should be dealt with first.

In every case the aim should be the most thorough destruction by the simplest methods.

If a sledge hammer will demolish a machine, why use explosives which might be used to make a land-mine?

The section detail to be prepared by you for your emergency use should set out:-

(i)   Name, make and type of machines in the factory and the method of destruction of each.

(ii)   Details of stocks of raw materials, and finished or partly finished products on hand; and suggested methods of destruction or rendering useless, if this is possible.

N.E.S. MOBILISING

New Regulations To Be Issued

BLACKOUTS EXPECTED

Authorities controlling national emergency services in New South Wales believe that if there was a Japanese raid on Sydney to-day arrangements for protecting the lives of the people would function effectively.

It is believed in Melbourne that the Federal Government will order almost total blackouts of the eastern coast of Australia before the end of the week.

The Minister for National Emergency Services, Mr. Heffron, said yesterday that regulations to be gazetted on Friday would provide that within 14 days fire-fighting equipment must be installed in buildings and that fire-fighters must be trained.

Mr. Heffron has issued instructions to the public on what to do if an air-raid occurs.

NEW FIRE-FIGHTING PROVISIONS

Mr. Heffron said that the regulations to be gazetted on Friday would provide:—

The owner of a building must, within 14 days of the gazettal of the regulations, provide fire-fighting equipment to deal with fires which may be caused "as the result of a war-like attack."

The owner must take necessary steps to ensure that in any building where 30 or more workers are employed a fire party of at least three for every 30 persons is provided. One fire party must be on each floor of a building.

Fire parties must be made available for training at any time directed by the Board of Fire Commissioners.

Fire parties will be trained to handle equipment to deal with incendiary bombs.

FIRE-SPOTTERS

An owner of a building must make available personnel for fire-spotting. Chief wardens will issue instructions to spotters, who will have to attend classes.

The Minister will be given power to direct municipal or shire councils, at their own expense, to allocate employees to obtain and supply sand to buildings in their area.

A schedule to the regulations sets out that each building must have the following fire-fighting equipment: Stirrup pumps (to extinguish fires caused by incendiary bombs); fire hoses; water; sand; long-handled shovels; rakes; and bags of sand in numbers to be determined by the fire brigade.

Regulations gazetted in August making it obligatory for owners of blocks of flats, office buildings, and other business premises, including mines and quarries, to provide shelters for workers and customers, have not yet come into operation.

They will, however, be enforced when a code, to be proclaimed under the National Emergency Services Act, is prepared. This code, among other things, will stipulate the Government requirements for a shelter.

It was pointed out yesterday that many firms in Sydney had not waited for the code, but had proceeded with the fitting up of "safety rooms" and other types of shelter in their premises.

All present plans for dealing with the effect of air raids on Sydney are based on the assumption that no raid could last for more than an hour.

There is accommodation for many thousands in underground railway tunnels round the city.

BLACK-OUT IN OFFICES

Black-out tests in Sydney have taken place on Sunday nights, and many blocks of offices have not made black-out arrangements. It was pointed out yesterday that it is the responsibility of tenants to black-out their own offices.

In city offices as in flats, the tenant must black-out rooms which he occupies exclusively. Blacking-out of vestibules and places used in common by all tenants is the responsibility of the owner.

Supplies of black-out paper in most city stores have been exhausted. It is believed, however, that stocks will be replenished within a couple of days. The paper is made in Australia.

INSURANCE URGED

CANBERRA, Wednesday.—The Associated Chambers of Commerce have urgently requested the Government to introduce an insurance scheme to cover civilian war risks.

Mr. Wilkins, the Federal secretary of the association, to-day sent a telegram to the Prime Minister, Mr. Curtin, asking that this matter should be considered by Cabinet after it had considered urgent defence measures.

WHAT TO DO IF RAIDERS COME HERE

Arrangements have been made throughout the A.R.P. area, which includes all big centres of population in the State, for all A.R.P. workers to go into as military and civil defence services will have urgent need for telephonic communications. The warden will attend to first-aid or ambulance transport being brought to a casualty.

(iii)   The names of members of your staff who have
been selected to destroy each machine.

A copy of this action detail should be forwarded
to your local Zone Control Officer for military
approval. (This plan would incidentally constitute
supporting evidence in War Damage Insurance claims.)

In all cases - remember that the enemy will
destroy when driven out or take valuable plant with
him - so don't leave him anything that he can use in
the vain hope that you will find it intact on your
return.

The State War Effort Co-ordination Committee,
therefore, on behalf of the State Government,
asks that you will give the most earnest and
immediate attention to the formulation of plans and
preparations which, in the case of invasion and of
military necessity, would most effectively deny the
use of your plant and materials to the enemy; and
also that having made these plans you will see to
it that those reliable members of your staff whom
you will have chosen to carry out the work are so
trained that, even in the stress of near-by battle,
they will do the job at the last moment Army order,
swiftly, effectively, unobtrusively.

Compensation:

Property owners who are contributors to the
War Damages Fund will be compensated for Scorched
Earth demolition; "War Damage" includes damage
(accidental and otherwise) occurring as the result
of the destruction of any property or goods for the
purpose of preventing it or them from falling into
enemy hands or being used by the enemy - as well as
damage caused by enemy action or action taken in
combating the enemy. Accidental damage resulting
from precautionary or preparatory measures taken

under <u>proper authority</u> to prevent or hinder enemy
attack is also covered by the National Security (War
Damages to Property) Regulations.

Contribution to the Fund is compulsory in the
case of owners of fixed property, plant over £1,000
in value, and stock-in-trade over £1,000 in value;
whilst owners of private chattels, plant or stock
under £1,000 value, growing crops, livestock or
agricultural fencing may participate in benefits by
voluntarily contributing to the Fund.

The War Damage Commission should be consulted
regarding plant and stock-in-trade of over £1,000 in
value, local government authorities regarding fixed
property and approved insurance companies regarding
private chattels, plant or stock under £1,000 value,
growing crops, livestock and agricultural fencing.

The limits of compensation are ascertainable from
each of the authorities mentioned.

DENIAL METHODS:

By Disposal:

Trenches should be prepared beforehand in hidden
localities known only to trusted persons, and well
removed from the workshop - the top turf to be
retained intact and the surplus soil indiscernably
scattered. These trenches are to be used in
emergency for the reception of such light equipment,
tools, parts etc. as cannot be previously disposed
of or are difficult to destroy. Particular attention
to the disposal of precision instruments and gauges
is required.

Alternatively, deep water should be located in
which to sink them.

If buried in trenches, tools, parts &c. should be
greased and wrapped to protect them from moisture;
the top turfs should be restored and the surface

camouflaged against enemy detection, e.g. as a
rubbish or firewood heap, or as may occur.

By Destruction:

Because of the scope of the field, it is not
possible to give detailed advice as to the methods
applicable to each special machine, and in any case,
it is not the intention of this code to teach the
expert his own job. It is essential, however, that
in formulating plans, special attention should be
paid to certain equipment, and the following are
notes in that connexion, given in the order of their
importance.

In all cases, it is essential that a complete
denial be made, organised simply, but in such a
way that an effective plant cannot be assembled
from parts collected from a number of partly denied
plants. As an example, if the distributors of every
internal combustion engine are destroyed, then no
engine can be run; but if every second engine only
is denied in this way, then half the engines could
possibly be put to work again.

Equipment:

(a) Machine Tools:- i.e. ALL metal working and
    repairing machines.

Lathes   - Smash pieces out of bed, with a
                sledge hammer, also smash driving
                gears, speed cones or other pulley
                drives. Cut lead screws, spline
                shafts and spindles with an oxy-
                torch or hammer, if time permits.

Drills   - Destroy saddle and drive, also lead
                screws, spline shafts and spindles
                as for lathes, if time permits. For
                small electric drills, thrust a
                screwdriver into the windings while

the machine is in motion, or cut
them with an oxy-torch, or smash
machine with a sledge hammer.

Milling   - Smash gears and, if time
Machines   permits, cut lead screws, spline
               shafts and spindles as for lathes.

Presses   - Smash frames, flywheel, arms
               and clutch with a sledge hammer
               or oxy-torch. Smash compressor
               on hydraulic presses by hitting
               cylinder head.

Grinding   - Smash head and bed, also
Machines   grinding wheels. With portable
               grinders, smash or cut with an oxy-
               torch as stated above for drills.

Shaping,   - Smash table and slides with a
Planing &   sledge hammer, and treat
Boring   lead screws, spline shafts and
Machines   spindles as for lathes.

(b) Power Units:- i.e. ALL sources of power.

Internal   - Drain or smash sump and radiator
Combustion   and run engine at full speed.
Engines   After seizing (which may take
               about 15-20 minutes) smash the
               distributor or injector. If
               circumstances do not permit this,
               smash cylinder head and distributor
               or injector. Also smash batteries
               and starting motors.

Electric   - Smash end cases with a sledge
Motors   hammer and burn out insulation
               and windings by lighting a bundle
               of oily waste inserted in the end
               frames.

Steam   - Screw down safety valve of boiler,
Engines   cut off feed water and build up

a large fire. Smash slide valve,
housing and cylinder with a sledge
hammer.

(c) Welding Plants:

| Electric Plants | - If power is available - short circuit leads of transformer, otherwise smash with a sledge hammer. Also smash torches. |
| Oxygen and Acetylene Plants | - Smash gauges and torches and release supplies of gas. (Be sure to release gas in open air.) |

(d) Furnaces and Forges:
Smash casing of blower with a sledge hammer.
Also smash switchboards, tuyere, burner, heating
elements, as applicable and if possible, damage
lining of furnaces. It may be possible to leave
a charge of molten metal in the furnace, in
addition to the above.

(e) Compressors:
Smash cylinder head.

(f) Charging Equipment:
Burst globe and smash stage switches.

(g) Retreading Plants:
Smash steam cavities on moulds. Smash
compressors and steam plant as stated above.

(h) Hydraulic Units:
Smash cylinder head and remove plugs on hoists.
Smash valves and pumps.

(i) Jacks:
Smash gearing or cylinder.

(j) Blocks and Tackles:
Smash pulleys and gear wheels with a sledge
hammer or cut with an oxy-torch.

(k) Precision Tools, Gauges and Hand Tools:
Every endeavour should be made to remove to a
place of safety, all precision tools and gauges.

Otherwise, grease well, wrap in cloth, place
in tins and bury in some place remote from
the factory. As a last resort - smash them or
throw them into deep water, e.g. a well, river,
lake, etc., or into a furnace. Hand tools to be
smashed, buried, or thrown into water.

(l) <u>Switchboards</u>:
Smash all boards and meters with a hammer. Cut
electric wires in as many places as possible, if
time permits.

(m) <u>Motor Vehicles</u>:
<u>Unregistered vehicles</u> that are jacked up should
be dismantled. Carburettors, distributors,
spark-coils, spark plugs, batteries, generators,
tools and tyres should be packed in a box and
properly labelled. Each part should have its
own label giving the name of the owner and the
type and model of the car to which it belonged.
The box should not be nailed up, however, until
instructions are given as to where it should be
sent for storage, as in an emergency it would be
necessary to destroy some or all of the parts, in
particular distributors, at short notice.
<u>Registered vehicles</u> should be effectively
serviced every evening, with petrol or charcoal
at the full, so that they can be used at a
moment's notice in emergency. But at the same
time the owners should plan to immobilise them at
equally short notice if the situation requires
and the Army so orders. Whatever salvage is
possible should be done in the latter case but
this must be subsidiary to complete denial to the
enemy.
<u>Salvage and Destruction before Abandonment</u>:
All vehicles should be destroyed in the event of
abandonment. This applies also to unassembled

motor vehicles in dealers' or distributors'
stocks.
Drivers or users should make themselves
acquainted beforehand with the given methods of
destruction.
Outside the city of Sydney, each should carry an
axe, suitable tools, and a bottle of inflammable
liquid.
Before abandoning, the vehicle must be driven
off the road out of the way - unless directed by
a military officer to form part of a military
obstruction.
If possible, prior to abandonment, the driver
should salvage spare wheels, tyres, tools,
batteries, spare parts and transfer them to
evacuation trains or motor vehicles, if any are
permitted by the Army at the time of abandonment.
Otherwise, he must irrevocably immobilise or
destroy the vehicle in the manner hereunder:
(Note: Denial of similar parts of every car is
        essential as the basic plan. This is
        to prevent the repair of some vehicles
        by collecting parts from others. The
        distributor must be removed from every
        car whatever other steps are taken to
        complete denial.)
(1) Motor Vehicles Without petrol:
    Remove or destroy distributor housing complete.
    Remove wheels, starting with spare - or slash
        or saw through tyres.
    Remove batteries, or smash with axe or
        hammer.
    Smash cylinder head with an axe or hammer.
    Break bottle of inflammable liquid or heap
        inflammable material over car, and ignite.
    If removed parts and tools cannot be salvaged

and transformed, hide, bury, smash and/or
throw into the burning vehicles. If buried
in safety, wrap in oily rag and place in a
container if time permits.

(2) <u>Motor Vehicles with Petrol</u>:
Puncture radiator and sump.
Start engine and leave running at full speed,
   to seize engine.
Slash or saw tyres, and smash tank and
   distributor after engine seizes.
Splash petrol inside the vehicle and ignite.

(3) <u>Motor Vehicles on Producer Gas</u>:
If producer is alight act as in (2) above.
If producer is cold act as in (1) and in
   addition smash mixing valve and hopper.

(4) <u>Trailers</u>:
Smash spokes, if possible.
Smash axle (including differential if any,
   and springs).
Burn if possible.

(5) <u>Tractors</u>:
Tractors are often required for military
works.
If not fully engaged on essential wartime
production they should be made available to
the Army <u>now</u>, if required.
On no account must they be allowed to fall
into enemy hands. If they cannot be hidden
beyond hope of discovery by the enemy they
should be destroyed.
Destruction on approach of the enemy must
be carried out - by one or other of the
following methods:-
(a) Drain sump and radiator, start the engine
   at full speed. After seizing, puncture
   fuel tank, smash battery and ignite;
   or

(b) Remove the cylinder head and injector
    complete and destroy - or wrap in an oil
    rag, place in a container and bury or hide
    in a place known only to the user and not
    discoverable by the enemy. Also slash
    tyres and smash battery;
    or
(c) Drop a stick of gelignite into the sump
    and ignite, then slash tyres and battery;
    or
(d) Run over a cliff.

(6) Motor tools and accessories:
    Break, smash, cut, burn or otherwise destroy
    or throw into deep water (sea, river or
    lake), or bury in a well concealed place.
    Smashing of electrical equipment, especially
    distributors, is particularly important.
    Batteries - smash with an axe.

(7) Unassembled motor vehicles:
    The engine and its component parts are
    separately cased. Open case and destroy
    the power unit, including carburettor and
    distributor with a sledge hammer.

(8) Motor vehicle spare parts stock:
    Smash with sledge hammer all fitments such
    as carburettors and distributors, batteries,
    car radios, etc. Saw tyres through in several
    places - but salvage and transfer or give away
    if at all possible - otherwise fire the store
    containing them, but only as a last resort.

(9) Aluminium, brass and copper parts &c.
    Bury at some remote spot or dump into sea or
    river, otherwise fire the store containing
    them.

(10) Bicycles:
     Bend or break forks, slash tyres, smash
     spokes.

(n) Stocks of Fuels:

    (1) Liquid fuels in underground tanks:-

If power is available, pump out contents and run to waste, or displace with water. Care must be taken to ensure that no damage can be caused if the liquid ignites while running to waste.

In any case, arrangements should be made to destroy the tank in the following way, in case time or circumstances will not permit the above method being used -

Prepare a piece of iron piping, 1½" diameter, sealed at one end, and long enough to reach from the bottom of the tank to the surface of the ground. For tanks about 500 gallon capacity, charge the pipe with 12 ozs. of A.N. 60 gelignite.[3] Fit the safety fuse and detonator and fill the pipe with dry sand. If it should become necessary to destroy the tank, place the tube, sealed end down, in the dip pipe of the tank, so that it rests on the bottom of the tank. Ignite the fuse and after the explosion, toss a bundle of flaming waste into the fuel and ignite it. If not full, fill up with water.

Bowsers:

Wreck the mechanisms of bowsers with a sledge hammer.

Drums, Tins &c.

Puncture all containers of liquid fuel (drums, tins etc.) and run contents to waste. If time does not permit this, keep as much as possible together then puncture some of the containers and ignite.

Oils &c:

All oils, greases, diesel fuels, etc. must also be treated similarly.

(2) <u>Solid Fuels</u>:-
Those fuels (timber, coal, charcoal etc.)
must be burnt.

(o) <u>Firefighting Equipment</u>:
Destroy in the following order: foam plants,
power fire pumps, water mains, static water
storage.

(p) <u>Telephone Systems</u> (private and P.M.G.):
Destroy switchboards and wreck instruments,
using a sledge hammer.

(q) <u>Horse Drawn Transport</u>:
<u>Vehicles</u>:
Smash spokes of all wheels and shafts.
Burn.
Remove or bury chains and other essentials.
<u>Animals</u>:
Any horses that cannot be evacuated before
military operations commence must be destroyed
if there be danger of their falling into enemy
hands.
All fodder must be burned or otherwise
destroyed.
All harness that cannot be removed must be buried
or destroyed by fire or slashing.

(r) <u>Stocks of raw, finished and partly finished</u>
<u>products</u>:
(1) <u>Metal Industries and General Engineering</u>:
In the case of large stocks of metals, it
would be a practical impossibility to destroy
completely. It may be possible to hinder the
enemy to some extent by firing the stores
containing these stocks, and this should at
least be done by generating an intense fire
made from old timber, oils, waste, etc., in
the store. Stocks stored in the open can only
be left, unless time permits their removal,

burying or dumping in the sea, river or lake as
the case may be. All timber stocks to be burnt.
With small stocks, burying, removing or dumping
in the sea river, or lake may be possible.

(2) Precision Instrument Industry:
All lenses should be smashed and all
instruments destroyed or wrecked by smashing
with a hammer or, as a last resort, by fire.

(3) Chemical Industries:
Run products to waste where possible,
otherwise throw into sea or river if time
permits, or else burn.

(4) Textile and Leather Industries:
Burning of all stocks should be carried out
only if it is impracticable to remove stocks
and bury or throw into the sea or a river.

(5) Electrical Industries:
Burn stocks or remove and bury, or throw into
sea or river, if possible.

(6) Foodstuff Industries:
Generally, foodstuffs can be contaminated
or ruined by exposing to the weather,
contaminating with creosote or by mixing with
some other substance easily obtained, such
as water, or sand, etc.
Only as a last resort use fire, and as far as
possible every endeavour must be made to give
away to civilians all stocks of foods which
can be stored or hidden by them. Only destroy
when it is impossible to prevent the foods
falling into enemy hands.

Additional Notes for certain specialised
industries:
Some vital part of every machine in the factory
must be removed or destroyed - that is essential,
and the following suggestions, under specialised

industry headings, are additional to and may be used
to supplement the methods based on the denial of
fundamental plant already given. They should be used
to make the job more thorough, and not as the basic
denial method, since the basic methods are devised
on the principle of the prevention of rehabilitation
by the enemy by the putting together of "bits
and pieces" collected from different partially
demolished plants.

If notes have not been included here to cover your
industry, prepare your action detail on similar
lines to that recommended for a similar industry.

If in doubt, contact your local Scorched Earth
Support Squad; also contact them if explosives are
required for any of your plant.

Foodstuff Industries:

Breweries, distilleries and wine industries:
Destroy stills, burst digester, damage vats and
run contents to waste. Smash all kegs, casks and
bottles and allow contents to run to waste. If
underground, contaminate with creosote.
Also smash motors of conveying machinery and
compressors and motors of refrigeration plant.
Smash some part of refrigeration system to allow
the gas to escape.

Flour and Rice Mills:
Remove and bury rolls in a remote place, or throw
them into a river, lake or well. If time does not
permit this, introduce heavy pieces of metal into
the rolls. At all costs, smash or remove rolls.

Dairy Produce Factories:
Destroy or remove all valves, taps and manhole
covers, on milk vats, cream vats, vacuum pans,
etc. Dispose of bowls on centrifugal separators.
Smash water and vacuum pumps by smashing

casing. Smash motors and some part of system on
refrigeration plant. Also smash compressors.

Abattoirs and Butcheries:
Smash compressors, motors and some part of system
on refrigeration plant. Smash vital parts of by-
products plant. Also wreck boilers, etc.

Sugar Refining:
Destroy boilers, centrifuges, vacuum plant and
vacuum pans. Run alcohol and molasses to waste.
Destroy distillery, fractionating columns and
stills, burst digester, damage vats and remove
taps and valves and bury, or destroy, or throw
them into a river or the sea.

Canneries:
Destroy canning and canmaking machinery, also
cookers and digesters.

Metal Industries and General Engineering:
 In some of the heavy machines, explosives may be
necessary to destroy the machine itself, but in all
cases, destroy the power unit of the machine. Smash
motors on overhead lifting gear and cranes or remove
stops from crane tracks, start up. Drain oils from
tempering vats and cut holes in sides. Smash valves
of steam hammers, cut the piston rod in two places
and smash cylinder. Power hammers can be used for
the smashing of essential parts of other machines
before being wrecked themselves. In electro-plating
works, remove or destroy anodes of special metals
such as nickel, chromium, silver, etc.
Destroy some vital part of every machine, in all
cases.

Sawmills and Timber Yards:
Smash saws completely - don't just smash teeth, as
these can be re-cut.
Burn all stocks of timber.

Ship and Boat Builders:
Destroy slips and crane mechanisms.

Toolmakers:
It is of great importance that as much of the toolmaking plant and equipment as possible be removed to a safe area.

Textile, and Leather Industries:

Boot Factories:
Destroy all machines in the clicking room, by wrecking the clutch mechanisms and drives. Also smash sole and heel attaching machines, and smash bearings and shafts on combination finishing machines and padding and brushing machines. Working part of each sewing machine should also be removed or smashed.

Leather Trades:
Smash vats.

Tents, Sails, Canvas Goods, Tailors:
Smash working part of sewing machines and cutting machines.

Woollen and Cotton Weaving, Spinning and Knitwear:
Destroy spindles and shuttles etc.

Chemical Industries:

Acid Manufacture:
Remove or destroy catalyst, and small ammonia catalyser.

Explosives Manufacture:
Fire raw materials.

Glue, Glycerine and Soap Manufacturers:
Destroy vats.

Optical Glass Manufacture:
Destroy grinders, etc.

Pharmaceutical and Chemical Manufactures:
Destroy reagents, retorts, vats.

Photographic Apparatus, and Materials:
Burn.

Rubber Industry:
Destroy rolls and vulcanising units.

Precision Instruments:
Destroy all instrument making and repairing
machinery and equipment.

It is the habit of the enemy to attempt first
entry in undefended or lightly defended areas,
converging thence on the fortified industrial
zones.

Denial actions therefore may be called for first
of all in coastal sectors, and preparation of denial
plans is therefore the more urgent for such sectors.

Obviously the cities will be defended to the last
street, but their complexity makes prior preparation
of denial plans also important.

E.H.F. Swain,

Chairman,

State War Effort Co-ordination Committee,

Scorched Earth Sub-Committee

14.11.42.

5

JETTIES AND WHARVES

Invasion would come by sea, with Northern Australia deemed the most vulnerable area because of its sparse population and its proximity to islands already occupied by the Japanese. But the east coast was seen as the most valuable area because government, the military establishment, industry and other resources were concentrated there. Ocean jetties and estuary wharves were therefore a key focus of the NSW Scorched Earth subcommittee. They made a careful inventory, listing 17 ocean jetties from Coffs Harbour to Eden that were to be destroyed by the Department of Public Works, including seven at Port Kembla and Catherine Hill Bay, with Byron Bay, Hawkesbury River, Lake Macquarie and Bermagui also on the list. They were ranked in order of potential importance to the enemy. Timber jetties were to be prepared immediately for demolition by explosives; access to masonry jetties would be prevented by scuttling moored ships or sinking concrete obstacles a short distance offshore as defenders withdrew.

Estuary wharves were also inventoried and assessed; a total of 149 were counted and their size, state of repair and ownership were meticulously recorded. Those able to accommodate large coastal

vessels were accorded high priority for denial. However, the
subcommittee decided that it was pointless to destroy them
because the enemy could still unload troops and materiel onto
river banks. Instead, artillery batteries would be placed within
range of river mouths and at the last minute, mines would be laid
in the channels.

DENIAL OF RESOURCES TO THE ENEMY
N.S.W. L. OF C. AREA.

Jetties and Wharves.

Ocean Jetties and Estuary Wharves (excluding the Port Stephens – Port Kembla Operational Areas, with the exception of the Hawkesbury River).

Military — Ocean Jetties would assist
reason   the enemy in his initial attack, and their occupation would greatly facilitate the landing of second and subsequent waves of troops and material and consolidation of the position.

Estuary wharves could be availed of for outflanking, infiltration and supply. The wharves of which denial to the enemy is more important are those to which seagoing ships can proceed and be accommodated. The denial of the smaller wharves is of little consequence. It should be noted that the destruction of estuary wharves will not greatly hinder the landing of enemy troops and supplies as this can be made directly on to the high river banks.

Mooring buoys could be used by the enemy in connection with berthing, but denial of these would cause little inconvenience.

Ocean Jetties:

Outside the defended areas there are thirteen ocean jetties (ten of timber and three of masonry) involved; they are important for denial to the

As beaches become battle stations ...

AUSTRALIAN militiamen are now at battle stations ready to protect their country. Here a gun crew is ready for action in a camouflaged position.

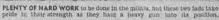

NOT MANY of these young militiamen did manual work in civil life, but they turn to digging-in with a will as they prepare gun positions at a battle station.

PLENTY OF HARD WORK to be done in the militia, but these two lads take pride in their strength as they haul a heavy gun into its position.

LOOKS like the real thing, this practice of a 25-pounder gun crew. Militiamen, drawn from every walk of life, are eager to take a smack at the Japs, who menace their country's freedom.

THIS JOB was a novelty at first to these boys, but now they're experts at doing their weekly wash in a wayside stream.

enemy. In some order of denial priority, these and their appropriate "Scorched Earth" <u>preparation</u> agencies are:-

(1)	Coff's Harbour	Public Works Department.
(2)	Woolgoolga	"
(3)	Byron Bay.	"
(4)	Jervis Bay (2 jetties at college).	"
(5)	Eden	"
(6)	Port Kembla No. 1.	"
	" No. 2 (A.I.S. Jetty).	"
	" No. 3 (new).	"
	" No. 3 (old).	"
	" No. 4.	"
	" Inflammable Liquids Jetty.	"
	" Water Jetty.	"
(7)	Merimbula.	"
(8)	Bermagui.	"
(9)	Tathra.	"
(10)	Catherine Hill Bay. (Wallarah Coal Co.)	"
(11)	Kiama.	"
(12)	Ulladulla.	"
(13)	Wollongong.	"

In addition to the above, however, there are two jetties in the Hawkesbury and two wharves in Lake Macquarie of equal denial importance, and these are with their appropriate preparation agencies:-

<u>Hawkesbury River:</u>

Long Island Workshop Jetty.   Railway Department.
Peats Vehicular Ferry Docks. Main Roads Board.

<u>Lake Macquarie:</u>

Swansea Bridge Wharf   Public Works Dept.
(owned by Lake Macquarie
Shire Council).

Coal Wharf North Bank near
  entrance (owned by Cam & Sons).   "

Estuary Wharves:

A total of 149 estuary wharves has been listed
and classified on consideration of the following
factors, viz:

(a) Depth of water at bar; (b) navigation
difficulties (shallow water, use of tugs, sharp
bends etc.); (c) depth of water at wharf; (d) size
and condition of wharf.

Schedule "A" appended shows the owner and
appropriate Scorched Earth agency in connection
with each wharf, while the wharves themselves are
evaluated for denial purposes on the following
factors:-

(1)   Good berth for larger coastal vessels.
(2)   Possible berth for larger coastal vessels.
(2a) Good berth for small coastal vessels.
(3)   Possible berth for small coastal vessels.
(4)   Little importance due to size, poor repair
      or lack of water depth.

Summarising Schedule "A" by rivers and berthing
values, it appears that only the Richmond, Clarence
and Macleay Rivers have wharves of first and second
denial importance, vide the following table:

River.	Classification.				
	1	2	2a	3	4.
Tweed.	–	–	1	7	7
Richmond.	9	9	–	–	5
Clarence.	13	15	–	–	5
Bellinger.	–	–	–	–	3
Nambucca.	–	–	–	–	2
Macleay.	4	10	–	–	12
Hastings.	–	–	–	1	3
Camden Haven.	–	–	–	2	–
Manning.	–	–	4	5	7
Cape Hawke.	–	–	–	2	4

River.		Classification.			
Crookhaven & Shoalhaven.	–	–	1	1	1
Clyde.	–	–	2	–	6
Moruya.	–	–	1	1	–
Wagonga.		–	1	4	1
Totals.	26	34	10	23	56

The small jetties and wharves within Broken Bay, Botany Bay, Frenchman's Bay, Kurnell, Bundeena and Port Hacking etc. as listed in Schedule "B" will be dealt with directly by the Army (1st Division).

Preparation:

A. Ocean Jetties – All thirteen ocean jetties must be prepared immediately for demolition, and instructions accordingly should issue at once to the agency named against each, through the Department of Public Works.

   The two Hawkesbury River jetties and the two Lake Macquarie wharves will be dealt with similarly.

   The ocean jetties at Ulladulla, Wollongong and Kiama are of stone. The depth is only sufficient for berthing shallow draught vessels drawing up to 9 ft. The only satisfactory denial method in the opinion of P.W.D. would be to scuttle a vessel in such a position as would prevent the use of the berth, or to lay concrete tetrahedrons to attain this result.

   The remainder are timber structures.

   The most practicable method of quick destruction of these timber structures is by the use of explosives. Burning would not be satisfactory; sawing and chopping would be slow and tedious; whilst destruction would have to proceed immediately, whereas with the use of explosives, demolition would proceed only on enemy approach.

Preparation therefore should be for explosive
demolition and explosives should be made
available. It should provide for the removal
or destruction of all repair material in the
vicinity, including timber stacks at adjacent
sawmills and depots, e.g. at Woolgoolga and
Coff's Harbour.

Personnel is to be organised at once by the
agency named and instantly set to work. (This
work is in progress).

Explosive charges should not be placed in
position until required but should be stored
in compliance with regulations reasonably
accessible to the work.

Action detail should be furnished as quickly
as possible by the Officer-in-charge of
preparation, to the Chief Engineer, Eastern
Command, setting forth:-

(a) Method.
(b) Explosives etc. required to complete
    demolition when ordered.
(c) Time required to complete preparation with
    the men available. (This action is being
    taken by the P.W.D. through Mr. Potter).

B. Estuary Wharves - Perusal of the classified
   summary shows that the more important of these
   are situated along the Richmond, Clarence and
   Macleay Rivers, as they permit navigation by
   larger vessels. In view of this and also owing
   to the fact that the enemy can land troops and
   supplies directly on to river banks, it appears
   that the destruction of estuary wharves would
   cause little practical obstruction to him.
   The mouths of these rivers could be protected,
   however, by shore batteries ranged on to the bar
   and by arrangements made to place mines in the

channel immediately <u>inside</u> the bar (such placing
of mines to be carried out expeditiously at the
last moment).

All cranes and other facilities on wharves
should be denied to the enemy.

Preparation for and Demolition Methods:

A. Ocean Jetties –
   (a) The aim is to demolish a section of the
       jetty, approximately 100' in length in the
       vicinity of the abutment of the jetty, or
       if the jetty has been constructed over a
       shelving beach then to demolish a similar
       section between the break in the surf at high
       and low tides.
   (b) Drill all girders in the 100' length at the ¼
       and ¾ points. Holes to be 1¼" diameter and to
       be drilled to within 2" of the opposite side
       of the girder and at 45° to the girder. If
       the decking is of timber then the holes will
       be bored from above through the timber, but
       if the decking is of concrete then the holes
       will be drilled from underneath from staging.
       Charge each hole with 2 plugs of
       $1^{1}/_{8}$" – 60% gelignite.
   (c) All piles, headstocks or capwales in the 100'
       length are to be shattered as follows:-
       (i) Jetty with headstocks –
           Lift decking where necessary and drill
           1¼" hole at 45° into headstock over each
           pile, the holes are to be drilled to
           within 2" of the opposite side of the
           headstock. Charge each hole with 2 plugs
           of $1^{1}/_{8}$ " – 60% gelignite.
           Also drill heads of all piles as
           follows:-

Drill 1¼" to 2" diameter holes
vertically into the centre of each pile
sufficiently deep to take the explosive
charges, using 1¼" diameter holes only
for piles of small diameter.

If drilling from the top of piles is
not practicable, then the piles are to
be drilled from the staging underneath
jetty keeping the holes well clear of
high water. The holes are to be drilled
at 45° into each pile and are to be bored
to within 2" to 3" of opposite side of the
pile. Holes are to be charged with
$1^{1}/_{8}$" – 60% gelignite in accordance with
the formula $9D^{2}$ (see below) and if one 1¼"
diameter hole is insufficient to take the
required charge, then two 1¼" diameter
holes side by side are to be bored.

(ii) Jetty with capwales –
The piles will be treated similarly as in
the case of jetty with headstocks.

(d) Fire charges with No. 6 detonator and safety
fuse. Detonators crimped on fuses are to
be prepared ready and each detonator and
approximately 3" of fuse dipped in "Dalco"
waterproofing compound, dried and placed in
magazine in a dry position.

(e) Charges to be tamped firmly into position and
after primer is placed, squeeze a piece of
dry paper on small piece of hessian against
primer. Tamp firmly with sand, damp paper or
small piece of hessian.

(f) Order of firing – fuses to be so cut and
lighted that girder shots will fire in
advance of headstocks, capwale or pile shots.

(g) A supply of kerosene has been arranged at
each jetty. If the timber is not completely

broken after the explosion, the kerosene
should then be applied liberally to the
shattered sections and ignited.

Note: For the purpose of calculating the
quantity of explosives required to
be put in the heads of piles, the
following formula will be used as a
guide -
If D = diameter of the timber in feet,
then $9D^2$ is the quantity of gelignite
required in ounces.
It should be noted further that 50%
more than quantity calculated above
should be used if there is any reason to
believe that the amount so calculated
is insufficient for any particular
location such as the junction of
several timbers or where there are iron
straps round the piles, etc.

The following preparatory work should be carried
out as soon as possible:-
(a) Drill all holes in readiness to receive
charges. A start being made immediately
the Army instructs that preparation for
demolition be carried out.
(b) Send portable magazines to be placed in a dry
position at the base of each timber jetty,
with the exception of jetties at Port Kembla,
as there is already a magazine at this port.
Forward immediately, gelignite, detonators,
fuse, fuse lighters, and waterproofing
compound to each jetty.
(c) Have "tails" consisting of detonator crimped
on fuse, prepared ready for use and packed
carefully in magazines.

(d) Train <u>at least</u> three men at each jetty in
the method of placing and firing charges
so that these men can carry out the work
expeditiously if the order is given by the
Army to demolish the jetty. Each volunteer
team should include, if possible, the
Wharfinger or Shipping Agent, all watchmen
engaged on watching the jetty and also if
possible a powder monkey. Arrangements also
should be made by the Army for these men
to be enlisted as members of the Volunteer
Defence Corps.

B. <u>Masonry Basins or Jetties</u>:
These are situated at Wollongong, Kiama and
Ulladulla and have been discussed with the
Army who agree that as these basins or jetties
can only be used for berthing shallow draught
vessels they should be left until all other
coastal timber jetties have been prepared for
demolition.
    The method recommended is to deny the enemy
their use by scuttling a vessel in the berth or
by sinking concrete tetrahedrons in the berthing
length, or by the construction of booms.

C. <u>Demolition of Cranes and other Facilities on</u>
<u>Ocean Jetties</u>:
Arrangements are to be made for the necessary
demolition of all cranes and other facilities on
jetties to be carried out by demolition squads.
    Proposed methods are:-
(1) Electric Cranes - remove motor or destroy
with hammers; remove and conceal essential
gears or destroy with hammers.
(2) Steam Cranes - destroy boilers by sealing off
safety valve and leave large fire under them

or place gelignite in boiler tubes or fire
box. Remove and conceal essential gears from
crane or destroy them with hammers.

(3) Smash jibs of all cranes by allowing them to
fall.

(4) Burn jibs or timber portions of hand cranes.

Note:- Coal loading machinery on No. 1 Jetty at
Port Kembla can be demolished by placing
charges of gelignite in the unloaders and
belt drives. Rubber conveyor belt should
be cut and destroyed.

Finance:

The operation is a "Scorched Earth" one under Army
Scorched Earth Regulations, and is an authorised
charge against Army Finance.

Actual Demolition:

Preparations must be completed as a matter of
extreme urgency against imminent invasion.

The actual moment of implementation will be
a military decision. Actual demolition will be
implemented by volunteer squads formed for the
purpose under Public Works Department supervision.
It will be done only on authentic order from the
Zone Control Officer through pre-arranged channels.

(Acknowledgement: Messrs. Potter of Public Works
Department, Armitage of Maritime
Services Board, Colonel Stewart
of Army, and Messrs. Westbrook,
Lane and Davis of the Forestry
Commission have contributed the
data on which this Operational
Plan is based.)

Schedule A - List of Estuary Wharves.

<u>Schedule B</u> - List of Jetties and Wharves being dealt
            with directly by Army.

                    E.H.F. SWAIN,
                     Chairman,
            Scorched Earth Sub-Committee,
State (N.S.W.) War Effort Co-ordination Committee.

23.11.42.

We must have the guts to hold on... and on...

History shows we have ALWAYS been at a disadvantage and ALWAYS won out

By LESLIE HAYLEN, News Editor of The Australian Women's Weekly

You hear a lot about the war in a week's work. I spoke for a moment or two to a general. He said, "We must attack!"

I quoted this to a civilian, who said, "What with?" But, as usual, I got the good oil on a tram.

"You know what I think?" said the man straphanging with me as he swayed closer to tell me his secret.

"THE ODDS ARE TEN-TO-ONE AGAINST US."

And he said it in great big capital letters, as long, as deep and significant as a pre-war beer.

HE was right. The odds are cruelly against us. But the remark set me thinking . . Is this the first time the odds have been against us?

I leave the answer to you. Just check up on our 150 years of history and see what the quiz reveals.

Governor Phillip took long odds on ever reaching the place—with his leaky old ships and his miserable cargo. But he made it.

He took longer odds than when he established the little settlement at Sydney Cove. The people almost starved. The food ships, when they did arrive, threw dead men over the sides instead of corn and flour, but axes grew keener and hunters more cunning, and we made it despite the odds.

Phillip took the longest odds of all when he said, in the teeth of the discontent of the new colony and apathy at home, "NOR DO I DOUBT THAT THIS COUNTRY WILL PROVE THE MOST VALUABLE ACQUISITION GREAT BRITAIN EVER MADE."

A brave bet for the father of a country to make on its first birthday, and what Australian, after 150 years, would not say that he's made that bet good, too.

These hazards against fate and nature are part of our way of life.

Isn't there something of Australia itself in our national password, "What's the odds?"

When I talked to soldiers about this aspect of the war it didn't seem to worry them.

Disturbed—worried

BUT the civilians were disturbed like the bloke on the tram. (Did I tell you it was a Randwick tram?) That citizen had panicked—wouldn't stake ten to one on a thoroughbred like White Australia.

That's where I think the soldier is thinking ahead of the civilian.

Out bivouacking in the bush, digging along the beaches, he gets the feel that it's a pretty good old place. He's not worrying; he's itching for a go at the Japs. He's got a positive philosophy. He's going to fight like hell to hold Australia.

Too many civilians you talk with hand you a necklace of negatives. They are weighted down with rumor, worried, suspicious of pep talks.

Mr. and Mrs. have a hundred personal worries—the boys overseas, the kids at home, time to get the backyard shelter finished—and the interminable, senseless, fatuous talk which all begins with "No"—no guns, no tanks, no this, no that—

In the words of the dear old sergeant-majors to the recruits who couldn't march straight, "You're a rabble, men—a rabble."

And wasn't the solution simple: you just had to keep in step, and you were an army.

Well, let us all get into step. Forget the things we haven't got yet—see what we can get—the best way to use them.

Well, what have we got? FAITH IN AUSTRALIA, SURELY. That's the biggest thing we have got, because on it depends everything. Being busy counting up the havenots, we are inclined to overlook the biggest HAVE—

Making it do!

THE second biggest HAVE we possess is something passed on to us from the pioneers. Making do with what we have —improvisation.

This nation was built on the recurring miracle of make do. When the pioneer's wife had no cloth for her man's shirt she made him one out of flour bags.

When the plough broke down and the nearest blacksmith a matter of 40 miles away, it was mended somehow, mostly with fencing wire.

The epic of Australia owes a lot to fencing wire. It mended the plough, the broken shaft of the sulky, it made a new handle for the billy.

Paxer and McIntosh flew to Australia in the early days of aviation in the most Australian plane ever to take the air.

It was mended here and there with fencing wire. The epic of make do again.

As in peace, so in war we must "make do."

It's ridiculous to say we have enough guns, tanks, planes. It's just as silly as to say we haven't any. We must make do until help arrives.

Let us utilise to the full the national capacity to find a substitute for something—or anything we have together and get into the fight. Let's make shift with other things until help arrives.

In this regard there's a fine recruit waiting. He's tired of watching us wringing our hands. He wants to get busy. His name is Native Ingenuity. He helped us out before—he will help us win this time.

We are being constantly told that modern war is a technique of surprise.

Well, let's surprise the enemy with some new ideas of our own.

Major-General Bennett, who fought the Japs, gives us a good start.

He tells us three things are on our side in the coming invasion:

Except for the narrow coastal belt, the Japs will find themselves on open country not suited to their infiltration tactics.

There will be no rubber plantations to trickle through, and we will know the terrain and they will not. We can make every tree and gully a little Tobruk. We can be offensive even in defensive positions.

In Malaya the Japs often wore sarongs, Malayan dress, and troops could not distinguish them from friendly people. There'll be no confusion here. We will know the Jap and go after him. He hasn't got a disguise to fool White Australia.

SO AUSTRALIA'S OURS—whatever the odds!

In Malaya they worked down the coast in stolen sampans, ducked under the mangroves by day, sailed on the next night, till they came to a good spot to land and get behind the lines. Here there'll be no sampans.

We can exploit the wat... problem as well as the scorched earth.

Use everything

IN Malaya the Japs had no water problem. Plenty of little streams and almost a daily tropical downpour.

Here they must land with water supplies.

It will be our problem, too, but we can provide for it in advance. We've faced droughts and won. The Japs must face a man-made drought, complete and pitiless. We must see to that—

Bushfires can fight for us. We can burn the enemy out.

We are versed in the ways of bushfires—to the Japs they will be a new terror.

The Jape had no food problems in the north. They found their staple food, rice, in every Malayan village or settlement.

They simply forced the natives to hand over their food and could carry on from there. In Australia that won't apply. They must bring their food.

How our guerrillas will raid those food dumps, the precious water reserves, the tenuous, cracking lines of communications.

Major-General Bennett says the Japs wither away under attack. We must always be attacking, always planning attack, thinking up new ways of breaking down the enemy—always breaking him down until help arrives.

And all the time our friends will be rushing planes, guns, and men to us.

Whatever the odds, we hold on.

IN AND OUT OF SOCIETY ... By WEP

SCHEDULE "A"
ESTUARY WHARVES.

Classification.	Location.	Owner.	Appropriate Denial Agency.
	Tweed River: (No coastal vessels entering as depth is 5'6" including tide over bar.)		
2a	West Training Wall.	N.S.W. Govt	Shire of Tweed
4	East Training Wall.	P.W.D. Coal Wharf 100 tons.	P.W.D.
3	East Training Wall.	N.S.W. Govt	Shire of Tweed.
4	Rocky Point	Cane Cutters' Assocn	Cane Cutters' Assocn staff.
4	Banora Point		Tweed Shire to supervise preparation.
4	Pelican Bay		
4	Terranora Ck.	Council.	Shire of Tweed.
4	Terranora Dock and Wharf.	P.W.D.	P.W.D.
3	Cudgen.	Council.	Shire of Tweed.
3	Tumbulgum.	Council.	Murwillumbah Municipality.
4	Condong.	Council.	do.
3	do.	C.S.R. Co.[1]	C.S.R. Co. do. supervise.
3	Murwillumbah.	North Coast S.N. Co.	N.C.S.N. Co.[2] do. do.
3	do.	Butter Factory.	Butter Factory. do. do.
3	do.	Council.	Murwillumbah Municipality.

Classifi-cation.	Location.	Owner.	Appropriate Denial Agency.
	Richmond River: (Max. of 1,000 tons gross with 12'6" draught, including tide over bar.)		
2	Richmond R. Head.	Council.	Tintenbar Shire.
1	Ballina.	Nth. Coast S.N. Co.	N.C.S.N. Co., Tintenbar Shire to supervise.
2	do.	P.W.D. Coal Wharf 200 tons.	P.W.D.
2	do.	Butter Factory.	Butter Factory, Tintenbar Shire to supervise.
4	Gerwan Ck.	Council.	Tintenbar Shire.
1	Wardell.	Council.	do.
1	Broadwater.	Council.	Woodburn Shire.
1	do.	C.S.R. Co.	C.S.R. Co. do. supervise.
2	Riley's Hill.	Council.	Woodburn Shire.
2	do.	P.W.D. Coal Wharf 80 tons.	P.W.D.
2	do. (lower).	Council or P.W.D.	Woodburn Shire.
2	do. (upper).	do.	do.
1	Sth. Woodburn	Council.	Gundurimba Shire.
4	Swan Bay.	Council.	do.
2	Coraki.	Butter Factory.	Butter Factory, Gundurimba Shire to supervise.

Classification.	Location.	Owner.	Appropriate Denial Agency.
1	do.	Council.	Gundurimba Shire.
4	Wyrallah.	Council.	do.
4	Sth. Gundurimba.	Council.	do.
1	Lismore.	Council.	Lismore Municipality.
2	do.	Foley Bros.[3]	do.
4	Lismore.	Gas Co.	Lismore Municipality.
1	do.	N.S.W. Railways.	N.S.W. Railways.
1	do.	Nth. Coast S.N. Co.	N.C.S.N. Co. do. supervise.

Clarence River: (Max. 750 tons gross with 12'6" to 13' draught including tide over bar.)

Classification.	Location.	Owner.	Appropriate Denial Agency.
4	Yamba.	Council.	Harwood Shire.
2	Iluka.	Council.	do.
1	do.	P.W.D. Coal Wharf 200 tons	P.W.D.
4	Chatsworth.	Council.	Harwood Shire.
1	Palmer's Island.	Council.	do.
2	Harwood Island.	Council.	Ulmarra Municipality.
1	do.	C.S.R. Co.	C.S.R. Co. do. supervise.
2	Ashby (dock & 2 wharves).	P.W.D.	Ulmarra Municipality.
4	Woodford Island (condemned 1941).		

Classification.	Location.	Owner.	Appropriate Denial Agency.
1	Maclean.	N.C.S.N. Co.	N.C.S.N. Co. do. supervise.
2	Kings Creek.	Council.	Ulmarra Municipality.
2	Woodford Leigh.	Council.	do.
2	Lawrence.	Council.	Copmanhurst Shire.
2	Woodford Dale.	Council.	Ulmarra Municipality.
2	Lower Southgate.	Council.	Copmanhurst Shire.
2	do.	Council.	do.
2	do.	Foley Bros.	do.
2	Brushgrove	Council.	Grafton Municipality.
2	Cowper.	Council.	do.
1	Ulmarra.	Council.	do.
1	Great Marlow.	Butter Factory.	Butter Factory. do. supervise.
4	do.	Council.	do.
2	Sth. Grafton (Piles and Girders).	A. Taylor & Co.	A. Taylor & Co. Grafton Munic. supervise.
2	do.	R.J. White & Co.[4]	R.J. White & Co. do.
2	do.	Brown Ltd.[5]	Brown Ltd. do.
1	do.	N.S.W. Railways.	N.S.W. Railways.
1	Grafton (above bridge).	Nth. Coast S.N. Co.	N.C.S.N. Co. Grafton Munic. supervise.
1	do.	do.	do. do.
1	do.	do.	do. do.

Classifi-cation.	Location.	Owner.	Appropriate Denial Agency.
1	do.	Frasers & Co.	Frasers & Co.
1	do.	Butter Factory.	Butter Factory.
1	do.	N.S.W. Railways.	N.S.W. Railways.
4	Copmanhurst.	Council.	Copmanhurst Shire.
	Bellinger River: (No coastal vessels entering as bar is very shallow.)		
4	Urunga	Council.	Bellingen Shire.
4	Raleigh	Council.	do.
4	Repton.		
	Nambucca River: (No coastal vessels entering as depth is about 5'6" including tide over bar.)		
4	Macksville.	Council.	Nambucca Shire.
4	do.	P.W.D. coal wharf 200 tons	P.W.D.
	Macleay River: (Max. of 900 tons gross with 11'6" draught including tide over bar.)		
2	South West Rocks.	P.W.D.	P.W.D.
1	Jerseyville.	Council.	Nambucca Shire.
2	Longreach (right bank).	Council.	do.
2	do. (left bank).	Council.	do.
2	Summer Island.	Council.	do.

Classification	Location	Owner	Appropriate Denial Agency
2	Kinchela.	Council.	Macleay Shire.
2	Partridges.	Council.	do.
2	Smithtown.	Council.	do.
1	do.	Nestles (A/sia) Ltd. Nestles.	do. supervise.
2	Gladstone.	Council.	Macleay Shire.
2	Seven Oaks.	Council.	do.
4	Frederickton East.	Council.	do.
2	Frederickton.	do.	do.
1	East Kempsey.	Council.	do.
1	Kempsey.	N.C.S.N. Co.	N.C.S.N. Co. do. supervise.
4	Euroka.	Council.	Macleay Shire.
4	Green Hills.	Council.	do.

There are nine further wharves in ruins.

Hastings River:
(No wharves can be used at present as it is shoaled up.)

Classification	Location	Owner	Appropriate Denial Agency
4	Port Macquarie.	Council.	Port Macquarie Municipality.
3	do.	P.W.D. coal wharf 100 tons.	P.W.D.
4	Wauchope.	Council.	Hastings Shire.
4	do.	Council.	do.

Classification.	Location.	Owner.	Appropriate Denial Agency.
	Camden Haven:		
	(No coastal vessels entering as depth is about 7' including tide over bar.)		
3	Dunbogan.	P.W.D. coal wharf 50 tons.	P.W.D.
3	Laurieton.	Council.	Hastings Shire.
	Manning River: (Max. of 300 tons gross with 9' draught including tide over bar) –		
	(Vessels have to be tugged in and out).		
2a	Harrington.	P.W.D. coal 60 tons.	Manning Shire.
4	Northern Training Wall.	Council.	do.
4	do.	Council.	do.
4	Southern Training Wall.	Council.	do.
4	Coopernook.	Council.	do.
2a	Croki (Jones Is.)	Council.	do.
2a	do.	Butter Factory.	do. supervise.
3	Oxley Island.	Council.	Taree Municipality.
3	Cundletown.	Council.	P.W.D. Taree Munic.
3	Cundle Dock.	P.W.D.	P.W.D. Taree Munic.
4	Redbank.	Council	Manning Shire.
4	Taree.	Butter Factory.	Butter Factory. Taree Munic. supervise.
2a	do.	N.C.S.N. Co.	N.C.S.N. Co.

Classification.	Location.	Owner.	Appropriate Denial Agency.
3	do.	Council.	Taree Municipality.
3	do.	Council.	do.
4	Wingham.	Council.	do.

Cape Hawke (Forster): (No coastal vessels entering as depth is about 5' including tide over bar – vessels have to be tugged in and out.)

4	Forster.	Council.	Stroud Shire.
3	do.	P.W.D.	P.W.D.
4	Tuncurry.	Council.	Manning Shire.
3	do.	Wright Bros.	Wright Bros. do. supervise
4	do.	Maxwell Porter.[6]	Maxwell Porter. do.
4	Wallis Lake.	Council.	Stroud Shire.

Crookhaven & Shoalhaven Rivers: (Max. of 300 tons gross with about 8'6" draught including tide over bar.)

3	Near entrance (Crookhaven Rvr.)	P.W.D. coal wharf.	P.W.D. or Nowra Munic.
4	Greenwell Point.	Council.	do.
2a	Nowra (Shoalhaven Rvr.)	Council.	do.

Clyde River: (Max. of 550 tons gross with draught 8'6" including tide over bar.)

4	Batemans Bay.	Perry's Spoke Mill.	Perry, Eurobodalla Shire supervise.

Classification.	Location.	Owner.	Appropriate Denial Agency.
4	do.	Mitchell Bros.[7]	Mitchell Bros.
4	do.	Fennings.	Fennings.
2a	do.	Council.	Eurobodalla Shire.
4	Buckenbowra Junct.[8]	Council.	do.
4	Shallow Crossing.	Council.	do.
2a	Nelligen.	Illawarra & Sth Cst. S.N.	I. & S.C.S.N. do. supervise.
4	do.	Council.	Eurobodalla Shire.

Moruya River: (Max. of 550 tons gross with draught 9' including tide over bar.) (There is also a secondary bar.)

Classification.	Location.	Owner.	Appropriate Denial Agency.
3	Granite Quarry	P.W.D. coal 80 tons.	P.W.D. or Eurobodalla Shire.
2a	Moruya Town Wharf Lt. Bank.	Council.	Eurobodalla Shire.

Wagonga River: (Max. of 400 tons gross with 8'6" draught including tide on bar.)

Classification.	Location.	Owner.	Appropriate Denial Agency.
	Narooma[9] left bank.	P.W.D.	P.W.D. or Eurobodalla Shire.
2a	Narooma do.	Council.	Eurobodalla Shire
3	Long Wharf do.	Council.	do.
3	Narooma.	Mitchell Bros.	Mitchell Bros. Eurobodalla Shire supervise.
3	Narooma.	White Timber Mill.	White.
3	Narooma Town left bank.	Council.	do.
4	Wagonga left bank.	Council.	Eurobodalla Shire

SCHEDULE "B"
Jetties and wharves being dealt with directly by Army.

1. Coal Loading Jetty, Bellambi.
2. Coal Loading Jetty, Bulli.
3. Jetty, Cabbage Tree Point (Port Hacking opposite Gunnamatta Bay).
4. Jetty, Taren Point (west of punt).
5. Jetty, Kurnell.
6. Jetty, Hungry Point (Opposite Cabbage Tree Point, Pt. Hacking).
7. Jetty, Bundeena Bay (Port Hacking, cast of Cabbage Tree Point).
8. Pier, Frenchman's Bay, La Perouse.
9. Botany Pier, Botany.
10. Jetty, Church Point (Ref.289428 Broken Bay, Military Map 1:63,360).
11. Timber Jetty, Church Pt. (Ref.292424 Broken Bay Military Map 1:63,360, ¼ mile S.E. of 10).
12. Timber Jetty, Stone Causeway, Church Pt. (Ref.303412 Broken Bay Military Map 1:63,360).
13. Timber Jetty, Newport (Ref.313411, Broken Bay Military Map 1:63,360).
14. Timber Jetty, Newport (Ref.413415, Broken Bay, Military Map 1:63,360).
15. Timber Jetty, Palm Beach (Ref.323484, Broken Bay, Military Map 1:63,360)
16. Timber Jetty, Barrenjoey (Ref.331504, Broken Bay, Military Map 1:63,360).
17. Bunnerong Power House Jetty, Botany Bay.

A mini-sub shortly after its recovery from Taylors Bay, Sydney Harbour.

6

WATERCRAFT

Boats would be invaluable to an invading force, enabling it to move troops and materiel up and down the coast or inland via harbours, lakes and rivers. Denying all watercraft to an advancing enemy would be extremely difficult if they were allowed to remain scattered around the state in private hands. New South Wales had roughly 25,000 watercraft, from dinghies to yachts and fishing boats. In accordance with national security regulations passed in early 1942,[1] all boats deemed to be nonessential (about 90 per cent of the total) were either beached above high-water mark or assembled at moorings guarded by the Army or Volunteer Defence Corps, which would destroy the craft en masse in the event of an emergency. (At one location in Lake Macquarie, there were more than 2000 boats.)[2] Boats that could not be monitored were to be disabled by removing oarlocks, rudders, tillers and engine parts. Where possible, the entire engine was removed for use by the Australian military.

Watercraft deemed to be essential—such as tugs, ferries, oyster boats and fishing trawlers—needed clearance to change their operating base or leave a harbour, and could not stay at sea for more than two days at a time. These craft were to be burned or scuttled in the face of an approaching enemy.

Conferences in March and April 1942, with representatives of the Army, Navy, the Department of Fisheries, the Maritime Services Board and the Scorched Earth subcommittee, established a special Watercraft Panel to coordinate the treatment of watercraft and develop an implementation policy.

DENIAL OF RESOURCES TO THE ENEMY
N.S.W. L. of C. AREA.

WATERCRAFT

Policy:

No watercraft must be allowed to fall into enemy hands to be used by him against us either in major coast-wise movements or in infiltrations from sea or river.

Non-essential craft must be immobilised; essential craft must be controlled and constantly attended.

Preparation for instant and effective denial must be made for both immobilised and exempted craft in military emergency.

Authority and Powers:

The authority will be the Minister for the Navy; or person authorised by him, to wit the Rear-Admiral-in-charge, H.M.A. Naval Establishments, Sydney.

The powers are contained in National Security Regulation 45D of 26/2/1942.

Under this Regulation, the authority may "prevent or impede the use of vessels ... in Australian waters"; by removing them upstream or from the water; or otherwise. Contravention is an offence. Authorised constables and Commonwealth officers may enforce.

Direction of 12/3/42 by the Rear Admiral-in-charge, authorised the removal of vessels, and mooring at places directed - by "the owners"; or, if he cannot be found, by the person authorised - and the "immobilisation, removal from water, or destruction of such vessels". Vessels in Port

Jackson are exempted. Exemption may be granted in respect of vessels elsewhere located.

Order of 10/3/42 defined and placed destruction (denial or "Scorched Earth") under the Chief of Naval Staff. It prescribed precautions for unattended vessels, i.e. by removal of vital parts.

The Regulation, Direction, and Order, assume to the Navy entire authority and responsibility for the immobilisation and denial of watercraft.

The operations were assigned to Captain Livesay, R.A.N., assisted by Lieutenant Pearson, R.A.N.

Co-ordination; Army, Navy, and Civil:

Conferences of 4th and 6th March, 1942, at the Offices of Maritime Services Board, were attended by:

Captain Livesay, R.A.N.
Major Pulling, Victoria Barracks.
Captain Ross, Victoria Barracks.
B. Filewood, State Liaison Officer.
E.H.F. Swain, Chairman ⎫ Scorched Earth
Police Inspector Standen⎭ Sub-Committee.
G. Faulks, Vice President ⎫ Maritime Services
R.S. Westhorp, Senior   ⎬ Board.
      Shipwright Surveyor⎭
T.C. Roughley, Superintendent of Fisheries.
J. Bennett, Supervising Inspector of Fisheries.
H.W. Atkins, Inspector of Fisheries.
D.N. Peterson, Secretary, Scorched Earth
      Sub-Committee.

Conferences of 10th and 13th April were attended by:

Captain Livesay, R.A.N.
Lt. Col. Perry, H.Q., V.D.C.
Major Wilthew, S.O., V.D.C.

Captain Heather, S.O., V.D.C.

Captain Garbett, Command Headquarters.

Captain Holman, Gll (Ops.) Base Headquarters.

B. Filewood, State Liaison Officer.

E.H.F. Swain, Chairman,   ⎫ Scorched Earth Sub-
Police Inspector Standen   ⎭ Committee.

R.S. Westhorp, Maritime Services Board.

T.C. Roughley, Superintendent of Fisheries.

J. Bennett, Supervising Inspector of Fisheries.

R.A. Frith, for Accountant, Fisheries Branch.

D.W. Peterson, Secretary, Scorched Earth Sub-
                              Committee.

The operational proposals which follow derive
from resolutions of these conferences.

Watercraft Panel:

The Conferences established as joint agency for
Navy and Army, a Watercraft Panel of the Scorched
Earth Sub-Committee of the N.S.W. State War Effort
Co-Ordination Committee.

The personnel of the Watercraft Panel was
constituted as follows:

(i)   Maritime Services Board - Mr. R.S.
        Westhorp.

(ii)   Fisheries Branch, Chief Secretary's
        Department - Mr. T. C. Roughley.

(iii)   V.D.C. Officer to be nominated:

The Chairman of the Scorched Earth Sub-Committee
(Mr. Swain) ipso facto became Chairman of the Panel.

The functions of the Panel were to:

(i)   Organise Scorched Earth Support Squads
        for Watercraft, the nuclei of which would
        be officers of the Fisheries Branch,

　　　　　　　Chief Secretary's Department, and of the
　　　　　　　Maritime Services Board.
　　(ii)　　　Develop codes for the control of
　　　　　　　immobilisation and denial.
　　(iii)　　Prepare organising instructions.
　　(iv)　　　Generally to supervise the organisation.
　　Subject always to the authority and powers
under National Security Regulation 45D and to the
authorisations necessary to be conveyed to it
thereunder.

Census and Classification of Watercraft:

　　A census of watercraft has been undertaken by the
Maritime Services Board, and a complete Register is
being compiled.

　　For the purposes of the operation, watercraft
were divided into:
　　(i)　　　Non-essential (pleasure &c.) craft.
　　(ii)　　　Essential (commercial &c.) craft.

　　There were approximately 22,500 craft classified
as non-essential. These were located as follows:-

Hawkesbury and Pittwater	3,000
Lake Macquarie.	1,800
Brisbane Water.	750
Port Stephens.	500
George's River	2,500
Port Hacking.	1,300
Lake Illawarra.	500
Coastal Rivers.	4,150
Port Jackson.	8,000
Estimated Total.	22,500

　　The estimated total value is over £3,000,000;
or, excluding those exempted in Port Jackson,
approximately £1,000,000.

Immobilisation of Non-essential Craft:

It was agreed that non-essential craft outside
Port Jackson should be immobilised by removal to
selected moorings upstream, craft under 16 feet to
be beached above highwater mark; craft 16 feet and
over to be moored.

Essential parts, as specified, to be removed from
engines which are not salvaged from immobilised
craft.

Funds were advanced by the Army for collecting,
towing and mooring, using boatmen crews supervised
by Fisheries Inspectors, Maritime Services Board
officers, and by Captain Livesay, R.A.N., and
Lieutenant Pearson, R.A.N.

Record has been kept of the boats so immobilised,
detailing owner's name, type of boat &c. The boats
have been marked accordingly.

This record will be kept at each mooring depot but
needs to be entered in the Maritime Services Board
Watercraft Register - and copies of the record for
each mooring are to be supplied to Maritime Services
Board for this purpose.

The Maritime Services Board will be the valuating
authority through the Senior Shipwright Surveyor
and staff, and in collaboration with the Fisheries
Branch will value each craft at each mooring,
recording its valuation against the particular craft
in the Maritime Services Board Watercraft Register.

No Insurance of Immobilised Craft:

The immobilised craft are uninsurable against
"Scorched Earth" if moored.

Commonwealth Marine War Risks Insurance applies
only to war risk; there is no authority to grant
cover against destruction to prevent use by the
enemy.

Hurdles under construction for the defence of Fremantle's beaches. On completion, they were tipped up and floated into position.

War Damage Insurance covers "Scorched Earth", <u>but only if the vessels are beached above high water mark</u>. For non-essential boats, owned as private chattels, insurance is voluntary. If the engines are removed, they can be insured against Scorched Earth.

The Minister for the Navy has under consideration the extension of War Damage Insurance to meet the position.

The N.S.W. Watercraft Conferences, after considerable discussion, points out that:

(i)   Voluntary insurance could probably not be availed of in the case of one-third of the owners now in the Fighting Forces.

(ii)   Compulsory insurance, after enforced mobilisation of craft over which owners now have no control, would arouse justifiable resentment.

(iii)   Insurance would cover only denial destruction and not natural deterioration

(iv)   It would be equitable to relieve owners of the cost of premiums as an offset against uncovered deterioration.

The recommendation is that the Commonwealth assume entire liability for the immobilised craft; and that maintenance, salvaging, and guarding be undertaken by the Commonwealth, both to minimise its liability and to conserve a valuable civil asset as a national obligation.

In the event of denial, the Commonwealth should assume the liability, without demand of premiums in this case.

Loss and deterioration are inseparable from the operation. (At Berowra, where 1,100 boats were immobilised, abnormal floods destroyed nearly 300 of them).

The Government obviously has a responsibility to return the craft to the owners in a condition

approximating that in which they were taken over, or
to compensate them for damage, undue deterioration
or destruction.

Maintenance and Salvage of Immobilised Craft:

The work should cover all reasonable precautions
to prevent foundering, and undue deterioration; and
where thought advisable should include the removal
of valuable engines to inland storage under Army
control.

Marine, petrol and diesel engines of small horse
power are practically unprocurable on the market,
and present indications are that this condition will
obtain for some considerable time, possibly for the
duration of the war.

Half the value of the boat is in the engine, which
will speedily deteriorate if left uncared for.

For both reasons, salvage of engines is a national
obligation.

The Navy or the Naval Auxiliary Patrol will
probably have need for some of these engines during
the war. The latter is already finding difficulty in
getting spare parts.

It will be necessary to take power for such
salvaging operations.

It is estimated that, under normal conditions, an
expenditure of about 15/- per boat per annum would
provide the labour necessary for the maintenance
of the pleasure boats now assembled at the various
depots. (This excludes Port Jackson where the craft
are of larger type and the cost would be somewhat
higher).

It is estimated, therefore, that £11,500 would
be required in one year for labour and that a
further sum of £3,500 would have to be found for
necessary equipment, in particular pumping gear

for use in bailing to prevent foundering and engine
deterioration from seepage.

Night watchmen would cost £3,500.

Removal of the more valuable engines, about 200 in
number, at £7 each, would cost £1,400.

Summarised:

Non-recurrent:

Plant and Equipment.	£3,500	
Removal and Storage of engines.	£1,400	£4,900

Annually recurrent:

Maintenance labour.	£11,500	
Night Watchmen.	3,500	£15,000
Total.		£19,900

It is pointed out that a recurrent expenditure
as suggested would be amply repaid in view of the
fact that the estimated value of the craft now
immobilised is £1,000,000, and that all would be
liable to total loss unless properly looked after.
The total number of boats involved at present is
about 14,500.

Proposed V.D.C. Maintenance Squads:

Conference agreed that whilst owners so desiring
might be permitted access to their immobilised
boats for purpose of maintenance (only) and subject
always to the local supervision of the controlling
authority or its agency, very few owners could avail
themselves of the opportunity, since one-third
were absent in the Fighting Forces, the average
tow-distance had been 24 miles, and petrol was
not available. In many cases also, access would be
difficult.

It recommended, therefore, the establishment of
Maintenance Squads of skilled boatmen, of suitable
physique, with preference to those whose living had

been affected by the immobilisation, e.g. boatshed proprietors.

These men wore to be offered enlistment in the V.D.C. for the especial purpose of watercraft maintenance. There would be at each depot at least one Corporal or other rank; affording appropriate pay equivalent to award rates.

Report was to be obtained of the number of men required at each depot, and the possibility of locally enlisting the requisite number.

The use of such V.D.C. Maintenance Squads would reduce the necessity for direct financial provision to £3,500 for plant and equipment, and reference to the Army for this provision becomes necessary.

Report was called for also as to the number and types of engines of 10 H.P. and upwards warranting salvage.

The V.D.C. Maintenance Squads would carry out maintenance and salvaging work as outlined in a code of instruction to be prepared and supervised by the Watercraft Panel, including:

    (i)   Removal of the more valuable engines and accessories to inland stores (subject to grant of authority).

    (ii)   Labelling all parts removed, giving adequate details for purposes of identification of ownership.

    (iii) Inventory of engines showing make, horsepower, and type (copies to go to Naval Stores Branch and Maritime Services Board).

Military Guards:

It was agreed that the V.D.C. should take over all guard duties. Local V.D.C. commanders would be called upon to advise the varying number of guards required at each mooring depot.

In the event of the V.D.C. being unable to provide guards at all depots, garrison battalion guards might have to be provided.

There must be a clearly defined line between the guards and the Maintenance Squads. The duties of the guards would be laid down by the Army.

Denial for immobilised boats:

It was determined that the Army should have control of denial preparation and operation, using the V.D.C. Maintenance Squads for preparation, the Guards to combine with the Squads for the denial operation.

Prior preparation was considered vital to effective last-moment denial. If preparation were complete, reinforcements would probably not be required.

The local Military Commander would direct the denial, with prior arrangement of lines of communication from headquarters to the Sergeant in charge of the guard.

Most of the craft now at moorings are in relatively shallow water, so that holing and sinking would not be effective.

As nearly all of the craft are of wood, the most effective destructive method, whether they be beached or afloat, is firing. This has the one disadvantage of attracting enemy attention.

Denial preparations should be made at once by having ready stocks of waste or wood shavings and a supply of oil, some axes should be available, and also a small supply of Molotov cocktails for mopping up. The Army will provide supplies.

Boats not afloat - Fire with help of waste and oil.

Boats afloat - These are in concentrations. A sufficient number will be filled with inflammable

material to act as "fire-ships", and will be evenly
distributed throughout the concentration. The
others will have smaller quantities of inflammable
material placed on board. When all are fired, the
"fire-ships" can be expected to provide such an
intense conflagration as to ensure the effectiveness
of the smaller fires.

Scorched Earth crews should be trained in
their duties so that the denial operation can be
accomplished expeditiously and effectively.

Control of Exempted Craft:
    Essential (commercial &c.) craft have been
exempted from immobilisation.
    These craft consist of the following types;
        (a) Fishing boats including Seine-net trawlers.
        (b) Lighters and punts (sugar cane and timber
            &c.)
        (c) Motor ferries and launches for passengers
            and cargo.
        (d) Oyster boats.
    In addition to the fishing boats engaged in
river or estuary fishing, or which fish in outside
waters adjacent to their home ports, there are
about 70 deep sea Seine net trawlers employed on the
coast of N.S.W., valued at £300,000. The majority
operate south of Port Jackson, often following the
fish and entering any available port or shelter as
circumstances require. Some were or are owned by
aliens, although now operated by British subjects.
They are thoroughly seaworthy, well-powered with
diesel engines, and capable of remaining at sea in
bad weather.
    On the Tweed, Richmond and Clarence there are about
150 sugar cane lighters, about 60 ft. long and 18 ft.
beam, together with about 15 steam or motor tugs.

At Port Stephens there are about 14 lighters of similar dimensions.

On various waters there are a number of motor boats 20-50 ft. in length, used as ferry boats. These vessels are often unattended, mainly during hours of darkness: the owners and crews reside a considerable distance from the vessels.

The oyster boats are 20-30 ft. long and of good beam.

A considerable number of small motor launches and rowing boats have been granted exemptions, and by direction of the Minister for the Navy, consideration is to be given, subject to security, to the possibility of extending exemptions in cases of hardship, subject to local immobilisation in owner's care.

At the same time there is reason to believe that non-essential craft in some cases are evading immobilisation by subterfuge.

Only such ferries, punts and commercial launches as are absolutely essential for the maintenance of communications should be exempted from immobilisation. It should be particularly noted that certain types such as log or sugar-cane punts would make ideal pontoons for bridge construction and could transport heavy equipment.

Where each or many of the members of a community own a boat for use as a ferry, the number should be reduced to one or two, even to the inconvenience of the community, and the others immobilised as in the case of Pleasure Craft. Competing passenger ferries should be rationalised, and the attention of the authorities drawn thereto.

The grant of exemption from immobilisation carries with it the obligation to prevent the acquisition or removal of such craft by unauthorised persons.

Those in charge of craft of whatever kind must
take full cognisance of the need to guard, or if
left unattended, remove essential parts from, their
boats.

Immobilisation should be the penalty for failure
to guard or remove essential parts, from craft.

It is assumed that any deterioration in the
military position will not be of such a rapid nature
as to preclude the possibility of some action to
deny the use of exempted craft to the enemy, but it
appears essential that the means to be adopted in
such an emergency should be formulated now so as
to ensure and expedite the removal of the vessels
to a pre-determined position, or arrange for their
control and denial.

Safeguarding unattended boats:
"Immobilisation of vessels order" of 10/3/42
applying to land, streams and territorial waters
affords power to the Navy to immobilise boats and
provides precautions for unattended boats, by
temporary removal of vital parts as follows:-

Steam vessels: Main throttle valve cover plate and
spindle.

Motor Craft: Distributor arm of the ignition or a
fuel injection valve of a diesel engine.

Sailing vessels with fixed masts &c.: Wheel or
tiller, or part of the rudder chains or screw gear.

Other sailing vessels: Masts, oars, rowlocks,
rudders; tillers and sails.

Rowing boats: Oars, rowlocks, rudders, painters,
masts and sails.

Means of scuttling must be available and be
applied by the owner at Navy direction.

It was agreed that these specifications needed
revision for Australian types and practice, and

details are to be worked out by Messrs. Westhorp
and Bennett in consultation with Captain Livesay,
keeping in mind the removal of identical parts from
power units of the same type.

The order promulgated by the Chief of Naval Staff
provides that all vessels shall be continually
under the care or supervision of some responsible
person, and this condition should be enforced. For
instance, during the sugar season it is the practice
for the cane lighters to be distributed throughout
the length of the respective rivers by tugs, and
collected for towing to the mills when loading has
been completed. During the period of loading the
punts generally are <u>not</u> under personal control
of any responsible person - it is possible for a
lighter to be unattended for some appreciable time.

It was considered that:

(1) During such periods as the lighters are moored
at the Company's mills, they should be under the
care of squads of the Company's employees in
watches to maintain 24-hour guards. The squads
so engaged should be men who are employed close
to the vessels; during working hours and at
night, the guards should be housed close to the
moored vessels. The squads should be instructed
as to their duties in case of emergency, and
drills should be held to ensure efficiency.

(2) Ferry boats and vehicular punts across rivers
controlled by the Department of Main Roads
or various Councils, should be attended
continuously.

(3) Wherever possible, small motor end rowing boats
should be hauled up well clear of the water
during hours of darkness, or when not employed
on service. Boats which cannot be removed from
the water should be moored as near as practicable

An air raid shelter being constructed by residents of Parsley Bay, Sydney.

to some habitation occupied by a physically
fit person, who would be charged with the duty
of ensuring their destruction when ordered to
do so.

Controlling Movements of Exempted Boats:
It was agreed that the movements of exempted craft
should be controlled, particularly in the case of
fishing craft that proceed to sea for days at a time
and do not always return to their home port; i.e.

(i)   No boat should be allowed to leave harbor
       without a clearance.

(ii)   No boat should remain at sea for more than
       48 hours, and

(iii) No boat should be permitted to operate
       from more than one base -

under penalty of removal from the exempted list.

It was further suggested that skippers should
have explicit instructions to scuttle their boats if
necessary, and that they should understand that this
must be done despite their own peril.

The Seine-net trawlers and other seagoing boats
should be placed under control, through issuance
of permits to vessels to leave port, during such
hours as may be determined, the permit to state
probable time of return, if return to the same port
is contemplated, or in the event of a fishing boat
proceeding to another port, the probable time of
arrival at the nominated port: in which case advice
would be forwarded to the authority at the port
concerned, giving name of vessel and probable time
of arrival. Otherwise reports of actual movements
should be given to the authority to be established.

Seine-net trawlers, as far as possible, should
only enter or leave port in daylight, but departure
and arrival at other times might be permitted

subject to provision for identification, the permit
for moving having been previously obtained.

Consideration should be given to the desirability
of preventing trawlers or other boats putting to
sea at all, after a chance of their capture appears
possible.

Conference recommended that power should be taken
by the Rear Admiral-in-charge, Naval Establishment,
Sydney, to implement control of movements of
exempted vessels in the directions indicated above.

Denial Methods for Exempted Craft:
In the case of craft exempted from immobilisation
there may be two stages -
  (i)   On the military command all such craft may
         be removed by the persons in charge to an
         immobilisation concentration point, as
         with pleasure craft.
         (Note: Time may not allow of this being
         done. A very special duty therefore
         devolves on persons holding exemptions
         to prepare for complete denial at short
         notice.)
  (ii)   Complete denial will be required, upon
         military command, when it appears there
         is danger of any craft falling into enemy
         hands.
         This may be done by firing or by
         scuttling, but the latter method must only
         be used in deep water where there is no
         danger of the salvage of the craft.
Prior preparations must be made if firing is
to be used as the denial method, and the means of
demolition must always be on board. No explosives
must be carried by passenger ferries, however,
whilst they are carrying passengers.

For boats on shore, inflammable materials, such as oil and waste or shavings, should be stored in a convenient place ready to be put in the craft and set alight at short notice.

For boats in use, similar stocks of inflammable material should be carried aboard at all times. Fuel in the craft's tanks will add to the conflagration but should be an additional and not the only source of the fire - tanks might be empty at the crucial moment.

For lighters and tugs: in the case of wooden lighters and tugs, action should be taken to provide highly inflammable material stored in receptacles and placed in approved positions, sufficient to ensure the complete destruction by burning of the vessels located at the mill.

During the sugar season when such lighters and tugs are away from the mills, each vessel should be in charge of a responsible person and sufficient inflammable material should be provided and stowed on board, to ensure the destruction of the boat should emergency develop. Managers should always know where the vessel is. In view of the possibility of destruction in midstream, a dinghy should be carried.

For the case of steel lighters, or even for the case of other vessels, a suitable demolition bomb will be designed by the Army and provided.

For Vehicular Ferries: A register of those vehicular punts in the possession of the Department of Main Roads, Shire Council &c. is to be made, and the authorities concerned required to prepare the denial operation and to train their staffs therein.

For Public Works Department dredges: Chief Engineer, Harbors and Rivers, to be desired to draft denial technique and to make preparations for denial.

For Power Boats: In the case of power boats,
denial by destruction of the power plant is of first
importance, and complete denial should include
scuttling in deep water, and burning.

Action Details:

These will be worked out by each agency or person
responsible for the craft, care being taken to see
that the denial squads fully understand their duties
and are properly trained.

The person or persons in charge of lighters, tugs,
ferry boats, vehicular punts &c. should be instructed
during off-service periods as to the best method
to be pursued to effectively deny the vessel, if
so ordered by competent authority, and care should
be taken that the person in charge in each case is
impressed with his responsibility in the matter.

Denial Moment:

The action moment will be decided by the Military
Command and will be transmitted to Denial Squads via
Sub-Area Officers and Zone Control Officers.

Denial Squads for Watercraft:

It is proposed that special Denial Squads be
formed at each centre for watercraft control,
policing, and denial.

These Squads will be organised and supervised
by the Watercraft Panel, and will be based on the
available local staffs of the Maritime Services
Board and of the Fisheries Branch of the Chief
Secretary's Department, with other co-opted
voluntary personnel.

Their activities will be co-ordinated with the
Denial Squads now being organised for country
centres, using Fire Brigade Officers as nuclei.

Their activities will include:

(i)   The instruction of owners in methods of
       denial.
(ii)   The preparation of a plan of denial,
       including communication and signals,
       for each control to be prepared in
       consultation with the local Denial Squad
       (General) and submitted for the approval
       of the Watercraft Panel.
(iii) The control of movements of exempted
       craft, if such be delegated by the Navy.

Legal Necessities:

To implement Conference recommendations,
authority in law is necessary in respect of:

Immobilisation of exempted craft:

An Order empowering immobilisation by authorised
persons, of all watercraft failing to comply
with paragraph 5 of National Security (General)
Regulation - Immobilisation of Vessels Order of
10.3.42.

And amending the specification of vital parts in
accordance with Australian types and practices.

Salvage of Marine Engines & Equipment:

An amendment of the National Security (General)
Regulations to provide for:
(a) Removal of engines and equipment by "authorised
    persons" - (being the persons for the time being
    in charge of the maintenance of watercraft with
    the consent of the Chief of Naval Staff) - or the
    owner, subject to the approval of the Chief of
    Naval Staff or deputy.
(b) Storage of engines and equipment removed, in
    such places and for such periods as the Chief of
    Naval Staff directs.

Denial Squads (Watercraft):

An Order under National Security (General)
Regulation 45D and the abovementioned Amendment to
the same Regulation - to provide for:

(a) The formation of Denial Squads (Watercraft) -
    to function as auxiliaries to the guards of
    "authorised persons" in charge of maintenance
    of immobilised watercraft.

(b) Empowering of Denial Squads (Watercraft) to:

    (i)   Police and enforce all National Security
           Regulations relating to Watercraft, and
           Orders and Directions made thereunder -
           for which purpose they shall have the
           powers of Commonwealth Police and
           Constables.

    (ii)   Control, at Military or Naval direction,
           the movements of all watercraft, including
           sea-going craft.

    (iii) Perform such other duties in relation to
           Watercraft as the Chief of Naval Staff may
           direct.

E.H.F. Swain,

Chairman,

Scorched Earth Sub-Committee,

State War Effort Co-ordination Committee.

23.11.42

7

PETROLEUM, OIL AND LUBRICANT SUPPLIES

When World War II began, virtually all of Australia's oil was imported. In mid-1942, the Commonwealth ordered the oil companies to form a pool—named 'Pool Petroleum'—to manage the shipping, storage and supply of oil for civilian use, which by then was strictly rationed. (The armed forces bought their fuel directly from the importers and stored it at Bulk Issue Petrol and Oil Depots, or BIPOD.) The pool's operations were directed by a committee representing the largest oil importers and resellers.

The pool directly or indirectly controlled hundreds of storage facilities, ranging from large surface tanks to underground tanks at petrol stations and piles of drums at rural depots. In the event of an invasion, oil at the smaller depots was to be moved wherever possible to the larger (Class A) depots, which would be taken over by the Army. If troops were forced to withdraw from an area, all oil stocks were to be destroyed by trained members of the Army or VDC. (Dutch and British oil companies had done this on a large scale in Borneo and the East Indies, wrecking and torching oilfields as the Japanese advanced.) The main means of destruction would be to open valves and burn the spilled oil or insert explosives into tanks. Where neither was feasible, the oil would be contaminated. The importance of oil for domestic and Australian military needs, however, meant destruction would be a last resort.

DENIAL OF RESOURCES TO THE ENEMY.
N.S.W. L. of C. Area.

POL SUPPLIES.

SURVEY:

1: ### The Existing Civil Organisation for Wholesale Supply:

Consists of a number of companies, dealing with motor spirits and oils, viz:

1. Atlantic Union.
2. Australian Motorists Petrol Co.
3. Caltex.
4. Shell Co.
5. H.C. Sleigh and Co.
6. Smyth Wylie (Aust.) Ltd.
7. Neptune Oil Co.
8. Vacuum Oil Co.
9. Commonwealth Oil Refineries.
10. Australian Iron and Steel (Benzol).
11. Broken Hill Pty.
12. National Oil Co. (Glen Davis).
13. Independent Oil Industries.
14. Associated Petroleum Co. of Australia.

and also the following, dealing only in lubricants, viz:

1. C.C. Wakefield & Co. Ltd.
2. Marrickville Margarine (Castor Oil).
3. Noyes Bros. Ltd.
4. O'Brien (Sydney) Ltd.
5. Wolverine Lubricants (Aust.)
6. Penn-wealth Oils Pty. Ltd.
7. Smith & Newbold (grease only).
8. Alfred Snashall.
9. Paykel Bros.
10. Regalin Aust. Pty. Ltd.

A cartoon playing on fears of Japanese invasion,
from *The Daily Telegraph*, 1942.

11. Lycett Pty. Ltd. (Castor).

12. Elder Smith & Co. Ltd.

13. B.V.R. Greatrex.

14. Ramsey & Tregalownay.

15. W.B. Dick & Co. Ltd.

16. A. Vale & Co. Pty.Ltd.

17. A.D. Hunter.

<u>Pool of Oil Companies</u> –

To rationalise the use of storage, a pooling
of the stocks of all companies has been
arranged by the Commonwealth Government so
as to release surplus storage at both bulk
depots and resellers' premises. The pool is a
marketing and distributing organisation only
and is not a channel for implementing denial
of liquid fuel to the enemy.

<u>State Petroleum Committee</u> –

There is an Army Advisory Oil Committee and a
State Petroleum Committee.

The latter consists of representatives of
the following major Oil Companies for N.S.W.:

Shell, A.M.P. Caltex, C.O.R., H.C. Sleigh,
Vacuum, Atlantic Union, Smyth Wylie.

There is no State Governmental or military
representation on the Committee – the
military authorities correspond directly
with the Chairman.

<u>THE POOL CONTROLS</u>:

(a) <u>Directly</u>:

    (i)   <u>Bulk Storage Installations</u>

Sydney	9	Total capacity	46,139,000 gals.
Pt. Kembla	1 "	"	3,350,000 "
Newcastle	7 "	"	11,637,000 "
		TOTAL.	61,125,000 "

    (ii) <u>Other Major Bulk Storages</u>:

Glen Davis Refinery –	1	2,124,000 gals.
Pt. Kembla (A.I.& S) – Benzol	1	514,000 "

```
                    Pt. Waratah, N'csle. (B.H.P.)
                              Benzol   1    496,000    "
                Granville (Refinery)   -  1  8,257,000    "
                           TOTAL.         11,391,000    "
```

(iii) "A" Class Depots:

District.	No.	Aggregate Capacity
Pt. Stephens to		
Pt. Kembla.	40	1,063,000 gals.
North Coast.	18	444,000 "
South Coast.	3	87,050 "
Inland.	161	4,372,000 "

The capacity ranges from 25,000 to 50,000 gallons. They are now 88% full.

Bulk storage installations and most "A" Class Depots are staffed by Oil Company Officers. Some "A" Class and all "B" Class depots are staffed by Agents.

(b) Indirectly:

(i) "B" Class Depots: situated in the smaller towns throughout the country and numbering 946; stocks held mostly in drums or tins, and represent about one-eighth the aggregate capacity of "A" Class depots.

Staffed by contract agents for the Oil Companies - mostly country storekeepers and carriers.

The pump equipment is owned in most cases by the Oil Companies, but in some the agent is the owner.

(ii) Reseller tanks and drum and package resellers:

There are 4,537 licensed resellers in N.S.W. of whom about 4,000 have underground tanks and pump equipment, the balance dealing in drum and package sales only.

Of the total of 4,537 there are 1,738 in the Sydney-Newcastle metropolitan areas – and 700 along the remaining coastal strip.

The number of tanks per station ranges from one to fourteen – the number of service stations per centre is much the same.

The average tank capacity is 450 gallons (leaving 50 gals. ullage in 500 gal. tanks) but since resellers now have to pay cash, the average holding is now reduced to 100 gallons.

CONSUMERS' STOCKS COMPRISE:

(i)   Army and Airforce dumps.

(ii) Commercial or Industrial Users' bowsers or dumps.

(Note: There are also 4,983 industrial pump holders in N.S.W.* of which 2,124 are in the Sydney-Newcastle Metropolitan areas and 406 along the rest of the coastal strip. Of the total of 2530 industrial pumps in the coastal area, about 406 are owned by consumers. Average pump capacity is 350 gallons.)

     * exclusive lower Riverina, part Western Division etc.

(iii) Small gallonages held by Motor Vehicle Owners.

NATIONAL SECURITY REGULATIONS AND BIPOD:
BIPOD is the Army organisation for the "Bulk Issue of Petrol and Oil Distribution". It will operate from the date of liquid fuel "mobilisation". It will take over all "A" class depots in declared areas, enlisting staffs of five

or a six men to each, and will service the
fighting forces directly. The following
is the general distribution of "A"
depots:-

Port Stephens to Port Kembla   -   40
North Coast   -   18
South Coast   -   3

PRINCIPLES:
  2:   The essential principles are:-
       (a) The use of burning oil as the chief means
           of destruction.
       (b) The use of explosives only when necessary
           and only as a last resource.
       (c) Removal or breaking up of items of small
           equipment, if time permits.

BULK STORAGE INSTALLATIONS:
  3:   E. in C's. Techl. Instn. No. 4 makes Oil
       Companies responsible for information
       regarding plans and preparatory work,
       which must be submitted to Comds. L. of C.
       for approval. Arrangements have been made
       through the Army Oil Advisory Committee for
       Oil Companies to commence the work.
           Co-operation between the Oil Companies
       and Military Authorities will be the liaison
       responsibility of N.S.W. L. of C. Area, which
       will also arrange for the training of key men
       in the installations and their enlistment in
       the V.D.C. and for the supply of explosives,
       demolition equipment and magazines as may
       be required.
           The general plan for systematic denial is
       sub-divided as under:

Dense clouds of smoke rising from oil tanks hit during the
first Japanese raid on Darwin, 19 February 1942.

(a) <u>Bulk Petrol, Fuel Oil and Lub. Oil
    Storage</u>:
    This is in steel surface tanks of up to
    2½ million gallons capacity with either
    fixed or floating roofs and sides encased
    in splinter-proof brickwork. The proposed
    methods of destruction in order of
    preference are:
    (i)   Ignition of the deliberately
          discharged content by stacks of
          inflammable material built in the
          compounds. These stacks should
          be protected from the weather
          and could be ignited by length of
          hemp rope saturated in kerosene.
          Alternatively firing may be by
          electrical methods, or by means of a
          Verey light pistol and cartridges.
    (ii) Flooding floating roofs with water
          through foam system to sink them,
          in addition to lighting discharged
          contents.
          In both cases compound bunds must
          be suitably breached, or channels
          or pipes from petrol tanks must be
          so provided so as to flow petrol or
          kerosene into the fuel and Lub. oils
          and thus assist their ignition. In
          lighting fires men should commence
          work "up wind".
(b) <u>Horizontal Elevated Gravity Tanks</u>:
    (i)   Without explosives: Open all
          valves, dip-stick fittings,
          vents etc. and smash them as much
          as possible. Allow contents to
          discharge and be ignited. Arrange

for a 2 in. valve at least for this
purpose.

(ii) With explosives: Place length of
1½″ dia. pipe containing 1 lb. of
gelignite for each 100 cu. ft. of
capacity down dip openings and
ignite; remainder of pipe should
be filled with sand. Tanks should
be three parts full, otherwise use
explosives outside.

(c) <u>Stocks in drums and tins</u>: (Also in "A"
depots).

(i)   When stocks are in stores, the
buildings are to be compounded and
flooded with petrol or kerosene.
Provide stacks of inflammable
materials which are to be ignited
by electrical resistance coils and/
or length of hemp rope soaked in
kerosene. At least two alternative
firing methods to be used. 10% of
the drums should be punctured.

(ii) In the case of Drum Stocks in the
open: a sufficient number of graded
channels are to be dug all over the
storage area, and drums of kerosene
placed at high ends to empty into
channels when punctured. Stacks of
inflammable materials surrounded
by drums of petrol or kerosene to
be suitably placed and ignited.
Mix drums of fuel and lub. oil
with drums of petrol in each stack
beforehand.

(d) <u>Ethyl Fluid Stocks</u>: Drums of Ethyl are to
be removed as first priority, or loaded

on punts or barges and scuttled in deep
water, or the contents poured out and
allowed to soak into the ground.

(e) Fire extinguishing equipment: Destroy
in following order: foam plants, power
fire pumps, water mains, static water
storage - smash this plant with heavy
hammers, and where possible flood with
petrol, and fire. Any floating roofs
should be sunk by pumping water through
the foam system before destruction.

(f) Pumping plants: Remove and destroy
vital parts. Fire a charge of 2 lbs. of
gelignite secured on outside of meter.
Wreck switchboard etc.

(g) Workshop and Garage Equipment: Destroy
machinery as directed under "The
Industrial Code".

(h) Petrol Waggons: Every endeavour should
be made to retreat with a full load of
fuel if ordered to do so by Military
Authorities. If this is impossible, run
contents to waste and puncture tanks:
otherwise pack a charge of 2 to 3 lbs.
gelignite around delivery outlet and
ignite. The truck engine should be
destroyed by smashing distributor and
cylinder head with a heavy hammer.
Demolition tools comprising heavy
hammers, picks, drum spanners, etc.
should be located at selected points.
Explosive charges should be made up, in
tubes or cartons and numbered to coincide
with marked charges.

"A" CLASS DEPOTS:

4: Under E.T. 1941 Sec. 97 para. 2, quoted in E. in C's. Techl. Instn. No. 4, the responsibility for demolition of "A" Class Depots rests with the A.A.S.C. which should request R.A.E. assistance if required. It is assumed that before the necessity for destroying "A" depots arises the area will have been declared "mobilized" and BIPOD will have taken over. Sufficient suitable pipe bombs as described in Appx. "D1" of E. in C's. Techl. Instn. No. 4 will be prepared immediately by L. of C. Engrs. and distributed to depots through BIPOD. HQ. N.S.W. L. of C. Area will arrange to select R.A.E. instructors and send them around depots to instruct staffs in placing and firing the charges. BIPOD is preparing a dem. plan for each depot which will give details of preparation and method of ordering execution.

When an area is declared "mobilized" POL stocks at "B" Depots will be taken over by BIPOD and transferred to nearest "A" Class Depot.

RESELLER TANKS:

5: The extent and distribution of these outfits makes total preparation impracticable and demolition by explosive charges will be adopted only in coastal towns in the most vulnerable areas. A contaminating agent is being investigated for use in reseller tanks, as an additional method of denial, and if adopted will be distributed through BIPOD. Its effectiveness is limited and it should not be relied on solely.

Where explosives are to be used, the
demolition is an R.A.E. responsibility which
will be delegated to V.D.C. but N.S.W. L.
of C. will, as required, assist in training
detachments and arrange for the supply
of necessary explosives and demolition
equipment.

Sufficient portable watertight charges
should be kept handy. These should consist
of an 8 ft. length of 1½″ dia. water pipe
charged with 12 ozs. of gelignite for a
500 gallon tank nearly full. This should fill
about 13 ins. of the pipe: remainder of pipe
is filled (tamped) with dry sand. Increase
quantity of explosive if tank is less full
and proportionately for larger tanks. The
charged pipe is lowered into the dip stick
opening until it rests on tank bottom.

COMMERCIAL & INDUSTRIAL BOWSER TANKS:

6: Methods for denial of these are set out on
page 5 of the Circular to Industries.

SMALL GALLONAGES HELD BY M.V. OWNERS:

7: Instructions regarding these are contained
in Citizen Code.

23.11.'42.

8

MOTOR TRANSPORT

By 1942 the Japanese were short of supply and transport ships. This shortage would be exacerbated if an invading force had to bring its own cars and trucks to Australia, as vehicles would displace weapons and ammunition in cargo holds. It was unlikely that the invaders could bring enough vehicles for all their needs. Depriving them of access to local vehicles was therefore a crucial part of scorched earth plans.

People living in coastal areas were urged to act immediately. Motor vehicle dealers were to offer their stocks to the Army—particularly tractors, which were urgently needed. Vehicles surplus to Army requirements were to be loaded with parts and tyres and dispersed to inland storage sites whose locations must be reported to police. Private owners in coastal regions were to send spare vehicles inland, using their own petrol rations to do so. Registered vehicles still in use were to be checked daily and kept topped up with fuel so they would be ready for use in an emergency—to help evacuate civilians or to transport Australian troops. Unregistered vehicles that could not be dispersed were to be dismantled. Their tyres and engine parts were to be packed up ready to be sent to a storage point or, in an emergency, destroyed. If vehicles had to be abandoned, their engines and vital parts were to be salvaged where possible for use by the Australian military. The vehicles were then to be driven off the road and completely immobilised or destroyed.

STATE WAR EFFORT CO-ORDINATION COMMITTEE.
Scorched Earth Code (Industrial & Services.)

PRIORITY E - MOTOR TRANSPORT.

Military reason:

  If the enemy can rely, as in Malaya, upon
requisitioning local motor vehicles, his shipping
will be relieved to concentrate upon munitions &c.

  He must be forced to bring his own land transport,
so as to intensify his shipping problems, and
increase his vulnerability - or alternatively to go
short of road transport in his operations in this
country.

  There must be the completest denial to him by us -
and the completest plan of denial instantly decided
and arranged now!

Denial Alternatives:

  Denial may be effected by:

  (i)   Dispersal.
  (ii) Immobilisation by partial dismantling.
  (iii) Total destruction in the last resort.

Dispersal:

  Once a district becomes the scene of military
operations, dispersal will be impossible, and motor
vehicles will be either impressed for Army use - or
denied to the enemy by destruction.

  Dispersal must be IMMEDIATE - or probably not at
all!

  (a) Motor Traders: The motor trade should at once
      disperse surplus stocks of new and second-
      hand vehicles, loaded with spare parts,
      tyres, and other essential materials - both
      locally and to inland stores.

        Each dealer should ascertain whether the
      Army wishes to acquire any or all of his

"There's something wrong with that bloke, Joe!"

stocks, and on that basis, decide what is
"surplus".

First attention should be paid to recent
year models.

(b) <u>Private Owners</u>: Privately owned vehicles,
either registered or unregistered, which
are not required for absolutely essential
wartime work, should be similarly dispersed,
if possible in the care of friends in inner
districts.

(c) <u>Petrol Rations for Dispersals</u>: Owners will
have to apply their ordinary ration tickets
to dispersals.

In the case of unregistered vehicles
or trade stocks, not entitled to ordinary
ration tickets, application may be made to
the Liquid Fuel Board for ration tickets
sufficient to remove the vehicle to a stated
place of storage, where the completion of
transfer must be reported to the Police.

Subject to Army approval, the Liquid Fuel
Board may grant such application.

In the event of special movements of motor
vehicles from one area to another being
required by the Army, the Liquid Fuel Board
may also grant emergency ration tickets for
such movement (Ref.41/M72/1316).

<u>Immobilisation:</u>

Traders, or owners of either registered or
unregistered vehicles should plan forthwith for
emergency immobilisation of any motor vehicle
remaining in their care in any vulnerable or
potentially vulnerable district.

<u>Unregistered vehicles</u> that are jacked up should
be dismantled at once. Carburettors, distributors,

spark-coils, spark plugs, batteries, generators,
tools and tyres should be packed in a box and
properly labelled. Each part should have its own
label giving the name of the owner and the type
and model of the car to which it belonged. The box
should not be nailed up, however, until instructions
are given as to where it should be sent for
storage, as in an emergency it would be necessary
to destroy some or all of the parts, in particular
distributors, at short notice.

Registered vehicles should be effectively
serviced every evening, with petrol or charcoal at
the full, so that they can be used at a moment's
notice in emergency. But at the same time the owners
must plan to immobilise them at equally short notice
if the situation requires and the Army so orders.
Whatever salvage is possible should be done in the
latter case but this must be subsidiary to complete
denial to the enemy.

Salvage and Destruction before Abandonment:
All vehicles must be destroyed in the event of
abandonment. This applies also to assembled motor
vehicles in dealers' or distributors' stocks.

Drivers or users should make themselves
acquainted beforehand with the given methods of
destruction.

Outside the city of Sydney, each should carry an
axe, suitable tools, and a bottle of inflammable
liquid.

Before abandoning, the vehicle must be driven
off the road out of the way - unless directed by
a military officer to form part of a military
obstruction.

If possible, prior to abandonment, the driver
should salvage spare wheels, tyres, tools,

batteries, spare parts, and transfer them to
evacuation trains or motor vehicles, if any are
permitted by the Army at the time of abandonment.

Otherwise, he must irrevocably immobilise or
destroy the vehicle in the manner hereunder:

(Note: Denial of similar parts of every car
         is essential as the basic plan. This is
         to prevent the repair of some vehicles
         by collecting parts from others. The
         distributor must be removed from every car
         whatever other steps are taken to complete
         denial.)

(1) Motor Vehicles without Petrol:
    Remove and destroy distributor housing complete.
    Remove wheels, starting with spare - or slash or
    saw through tyres.
    Remove batteries or smash with axe or hammer.
    Smash cylinder head.
    Break bottle of inflammable liquid or heap
    inflammable material over car; and ignite.
    If removed parts and tools cannot be salvaged
    and transferred, hide, bury, smash and/or throw
    into the burning vehicles. If buried in safety,
    wrap in oily rag and place in a container if time
    permits.

(2) Motor Vehicles with Petrol:
    Puncture radiator and sump.
    Start engine and leave running at full speed, to
    seize engine.
    Slash or saw tyres, and smash petrol tank and
    distributor after engine seizes.
    Splash petrol inside the vehicle and ignite.

(3) Motor Vehicles on Producer Gas:
    If producer is alight act as in (2) above.
    If producer is cold act as in (1) and in addition
    smash mixing valve and hopper.

(4) <u>Trailers</u>:

Smash spokes.

Smash axle (including differential if any, and springs). Burn if possible.

(5) <u>Tractors</u>:

Tractors are indispensable for military works and are urgently required.

If not fully engaged on essential wartime production they should be made available to the Army <u>now</u> - or dispersed from the coastal areas. On no account must they be allowed to fall into enemy hands.

Destruction on approach of the enemy must be carried out - by one or other of the following methods:

(a) Drain sump and radiator, start the engine at full speed - then:
    Puncture fuel tank, and ignite;
       or:

(b) Remove the distributor housing complete and destroy - or wrap in an oil rag, place in a container and bury or hide in a place known only to the user and not discoverable by the enemy;
       or:

(c) Drop a stick of gelignite into the sump and ignite;
       or:

(d) Run over a cliff.

If not on essential work, tractors should be evacuated from coastal areas or handed over to the Military NOW.

(6) <u>Motor tools and accessories</u>:

Break, smash, cut, burn or otherwise destroy or throw into deep water (sea, river or lake), or bury in a well concealed place. Smashing of

electrical equipment, especially distributors,
is particularly important.
Batteries – smash with an axe.

Compensation:

(i)   No compensation can be claimed for loss due
       to destruction under the Scorched Earth
       plan unless the owner has availed himself of
       the War Damage Insurance scheme. You should
       take precautions now and see that you have a
       proper cover.

(ii)   Vehicles and spare parts will be paid for if
       taken over by the Army prior to application
       of a Scorched Earth plan.

25.3.'42

Coal-powered gas producer plants were attached to motor vehicles to save fuel for industry and military.

9

MOTOR REPAIR EQUIPMENT

If Australian vehicles were kept out of Japanese hands and the invaders were forced to import their own, they would need equipment and tools to maintain and repair them. Similarly, motors used in industry also required regular maintenance and repair. Tools and equipment for all kinds of motor repairs were to be dispersed, destroyed or hidden by the citizenry before they evacuated a given location. The items in question ranged from precision instruments to lathes, welding equipment, furnaces and power units. Small items such as tools, gauges and machine parts that would be difficult or costly to replace were to be buried in well-camouflaged trenches or sunk in deep water. Other items would have their essential components smashed. Each repair facility was to prepare its own plan and nominate skilled and trusted staff to carry out the tasks involved.

Hyde Park Air Raid Shelter, Sydney.

STATE WAR EFFORT CO-ORDINATION COMMITTEE.
Scorched Earth Code (Industrial & Services).

PRIORITY F: MOTOR &c. REPAIR EQUIPMENT, TOOLS, SPARE PARTS &c.

This priority covers machines, equipment, tools and spare parts &c. in garages and workshops, whether Governmental, trade, taxi-company, private &c.; it includes spare and utilisable parts in car 'graveyards'.

Military reason:

It is vitally important that local facilities for the repair of enemy vehicles, machinery and equipment be denied to the enemy by prior disposal or demolition.

The employer or management on the one hand, the employee or user-in-possession on the other will be responsible for denying such facilities to the enemy.

Service must continue to the last possible hour but each employer or management should prepare a plan of denial immediately, and issue to his employees instructions on arrangements and methods for last moment denial by disposal or destruction of all things likely to be of use to the enemy. These should state the name of the employee responsible for the execution of each job, and the method of denial.

A copy of the prior plan of denial containing the instructions should be lodged with the Department of Road Transport, which is the supervising agency of the State War Effort Co-Ordination Committee in this field. This plan will be supporting evidence in War Damage Insurance claims.

DENIAL METHODS:

By Disposal:

Trenches should be prepared beforehand in hidden
localities known only to trusted persons, and well
removed from the workshop - the top turf to be
retained intact and the surplus soil indiscernably
scattered. These trenches are to be used in
emergency for the reception of such light equipment,
tools, parts etc. as cannot be previously disposed
of or are difficult to destroy. Particular attention
to the disposal of precision instruments and gauges
is required.

Alternatively, deep water should be located in
which to sink them.

If buried in trenches, tools, parts &c. should be
greased and wrapped to protect them from moisture;
the top turfs should be restored and the surface
camouflaged against enemy detection, e.g. as a
rubbish or firewood heap, or as may occur.

By Destruction:

Because of the scope of the field, it is not
possible to give detailed advice as to the methods
applicable to each special machine, and in any case,
it is not the intention of this code to teach the
expert his own job. It is essential, however, that
in formulating plans, special attention should be
paid to certain equipment, and the following are
notes in that connection, given in the order of
their importance.

In all cases, it is essential that a complete
denial be made, organised simply, but in such a
way that an effective plant cannot be assembled
from parts collected from a number of partly denied
plants. As an example, if the distributors of every

internal combustion engine are destroyed, then no
engine can be run; but if every second engine only
is denied in this way, then half the engines could
possibly be put to work again.

Equipment:
(a) <u>Machine Tools</u>:- i.e. <u>ALL</u> metal working and
   repairing machines.
   Lathes -   Smash pieces out of bed, with a sledge
               hammer, also smash driving gears,
               speed cones or other pulley drives.
   Drills -   Destroy saddle and drive on large
               machines. For small electric drills,
               thrust a screwdriver into the windings
               while the machine is in motion, or
               cut them with an oxy-torch, or smash
               machine with a sledge hammer.
   Presses -   Smash flywheel, arms and clutch with
               a sledge hammer or oxy-torch. Smash
               compressor on hydraulic presses by
               hitting cylinder head.
   Shaping Machines -   Smash slides and crank with
                        a sledge hammer.
   Planing Machines -   Smash gearing, drive and
                        bed.
   Milling Machines -   Smash drive.
   Grinding Machines - Smash head and bed, also
                        grinding wheels. With
                        portable grinders, smash
                        or cut with an oxy-torch as
                        stated above for drills.
(b) <u>Power Units</u>:- i.e. <u>ALL</u> sources of power.
   Internal combustion engines - drain or smash
         sump and radiator and run engine at full
         speed. After seizing (which may take about
         15-20 minutes) smash the distributor or

injector. If circumstances do not permit
this, smash cylinder head and distributor
or injector. Also smash batteries and
starting motors.

Electric Motors - smash end cases with a sledge
hammer and burn out insulation and windings
by lighting a bundle of oily waste inserted
in the end frames.

Steam Engines - Screw down safety valve, cut off
feed water and build up a large fire.

(c) Welding plants:

Electric Plants - If power is available - short
circuit leads of transformer, otherwise
smash with a sledge hammer. Also smash
torches.

Oxygen and Acetylene Plants - smash gauges and
torches and release supplies of gas. (Be
sure to release gas in open air).

(d) Furnaces and Forges:

Smash blower with a sledge hammer. Also smash
tuyere, burner, heating elements, as applicable
and if possible, damage lining of furnaces. It
may be possible to leave a charge of molten metal
in the furnace, in addition to the above.

(e) Compressors:

Smash cylinder head.

(f) Charging Equipment:

Burst globe and smash stage switches.

(g) Retreading Plants:

Smash steam cavities on moulds. Smash
compressors and steam plant as stated above.

(h) Hoists:

Smash cylinder head and remove plugs.

(i) Jacks:

Smash gearing or cylinder.

(j) <u>Blocks and Tackles</u>:
   Smash pulleys and gear wheels with a sledge
   hammer or cut with an oxy-torch.

(k) <u>Precision Tools, Gauges and Hand Tools</u>:
   Every endeavour should be made to remove to a
   place of safety, all precision tools and gauges.
   Otherwise, grease well, wrap in cloth, place
   in tins and bury in some place remote from the
   factory. As a last resort - smash them or throw
   them into deep water, e.g. a well, river or lake.
   Hand tools to be smashed, buried, or thrown into
   water.

<u>Spare Parts Stock</u>:

(a) <u>Unassembled motor vehicles</u>:
   The engine and its component parts are separately
   cased. Open case and destroy the power unit,
   including carburettor and distributor with a
   sledge hammer.

(b) <u>Spare parts stock</u>:
   Smash with sledge hammer power units, and all
   fitments such as carburettors and distributors,
   batteries, car radios.

(c) <u>Tyres</u>:
   Saw through in several places - but salvage and
   transfer or give away if at all possible.

(d) <u>Producer Gas Plants</u>:
   Smash mixing valve and hopper.

(e) <u>Aluminium, brass and copper parts</u>:
   Bury at some remote spot or dump into sea or
   river.
   If time does not permit the smashing and/or
   burying of spare parts stock, use fire, but only
   as a last resort.

Action Moment:

The denial command will be issued by the local
Army authorities, and will obviously be issued only
if danger is imminent and enemy pressure critical.
Little time will remain for the implementation of
the prepared Action detail and the selected staff
must hold themselves in readiness to receive the
Army order from known Military, Police or Scorched
Earth Support Squad messengers.

If enemy approach is obvious, and Army
message fails to arrive, action should be taken
nevertheless.

30.3.'42.

10

COAL MINES

Although most Allied and Japanese naval shipping ran on oil, most Australian merchant ships were coal-fired. If the abundant supplies of black coal in New South Wales and Queensland were left intact, invaders might use them to fuel captured vessels and transport troops and supplies along coasts or rivers. (Japan's remoteness and the shortage of Japanese cargo ships made it unlikely that coal would be exported to the home islands.) The NSW Scorched Earth subcommittee was determined to prevent this. Selected personnel at all coal mines were given responsibility for a range of measures to render mines unusable, including the removal or destruction of equipment and infrastructure and the use of explosives to collapse tunnel entrances. The aim was to keep coal out of the hands of invaders while ensuring that mines could be brought back into production relatively quickly after the war.

<u>DENIAL OF RESOURCES TO THE ENEMY</u>
<u>N.S.W. L. of C. AREA.</u>

<u>COAL MINES.</u>

<u>Military reasons</u>: Coal is essential to shipping; and to occupation and should be denied to the enemy.

<u>Census of Mines</u>: The majority of the coal mines in N.S.W. are in four main districts viz:

(i)   Maitland-Cessnock.

(ii) Newcastle.

(iii) South Coast.

(iv) Western-Lithgow-
      Wallerawang-Mudgee.

There are coal mines also at Liddell, Muswellbrook, Gunnedah, Werris Creek and other centres in the North West; at East Maitland and Beresford; and at Berrima and in the Burragorang Valley. Schedule attached, lists names and addresses of the coal mines, owner, Secretary, head office, Manager, Under Manager, certificated electrician, and the District Inspector of Collieries; the mine telephone number, whether the mine is a "shaft" or "tunnel" mine, large, or small, and in the case of large mines, the number of persons employed.

State War Effort Co-ordination Committee (Scorched
Earth) Operational Plan Agency:

> Department of Mines; using
> its District Inspectors of
> Collieries, each of whom become
> the Coal Mining "Scorched Earth"
> representative, functioning
> under Army Scorched Earth
> National Security Regulations.

Operational Plan Principles:

> The object of the plan is to
> deny to the enemy the use of
> the mine for the entire period
> of any possible occupation of
> the district; and to organise
> beforehand for a last-moment
> implementation of the plan
> of denials at emergency
> military signal and command,
> authentically conveyed by the
> local military command through
> the District Inspector of
> Collieries to the manager of each
> mine.

Denial Methods:

> The suggested methods of denial
> are as follows:-
> Salvage and removal - to a
> previously selected place, if
> possible - of:
> (i)   Horses.
> (ii)   Safety lamps.
> (iii) Mine plans and colliery
>   records.
> (iv)   Telephones, cables, motors,
>   tools, ambulance and rescue
>   appliances and other

apparatus that may be of
military value.

(v) Railway locomotives and
rolling stock.

(vi) Essential parts of
machinery, such as the
armature of exciters for
turbines, boiler feed pump
valves, etc.

Destruction of:

(i) Items under "salvage and
removal" which cannot in
emergency be so disposed of;

(ii) Winding headgear - to
be cut near the base and
pulled over.

(iii) Guide and winding ropes -
to be cut and allowed to
fall down the shaft.

(iv) The wooden portion of
gantries, stores that
cannot be removed, surface
buildings, skips and other
inflammable material on the
surface - to be fired.

(v) Steel or concrete gantry
supports - to be subject
to effective explosive
charges.

(vi) Electrical apparatus,
underground motors and
other appliances - to be
destroyed with a sledge
hammer, fire or explosives.

(vii) Ventilating fans - to be
destroyed by removal and/or
destruction of bearings.

(viii) Supports for overhead
transmission lines - to
be fired or destroyed by
explosives.

(ix) Surplus explosives which
cannot be removed - to be
destroyed.

(x) Portions of roofs at the
vicinity of tunnel mouths -
to be brought down, by
removal of roof supports
or by explosives set in
the roof.

Action details for each Mine:

District Inspector of Collieries should
confer with the Manager of each mine seeking his
collaboration with the Army, and with the State
War Effort Co-Ordination Committee, in the instant
preparation of a Scorched Earth Action Detail for
each mine, on the lines suggested under "Denial
Methods", and in the prior organisation of personnel
trained ready for last-moment action in military
emergency.

The personnel should be volunteers, carefully
selected by the Manager for such anti-enemy last-
moment action as cool, quick and reliable.

They should be given whatever prior instruction
and preparation may be possible.

Their names, addresses and occupations, and the
denial duties they are to perform, should be made
available to the District Inspector of Collieries
acting as Mining District Scorched Earth authority.

Action moment:

   The action moment will be decided by the local
Army Command. Obviously it will not issue until
emergency is imminent, and enemy pressure critical.
Little time will remain for implementation of
the prepared Action Detail, and the Scorched
Earth personnel of the mine should hold itself in
readiness to receive the Army order through the
District Inspector of Collieries.

(Acknowledgement: The data for the plan has been
                        prepared by P.W. Hay, Esq.,
                        Chief Inspector of Mines, in
                        collaboration with A.N. Graham,
                        Esq., Under Secretary for Mines.)

                        E.H.F. Swain.
                         Chairman.
     State War Effort Co-Ordination Committee,
          Scorched Earth Sub-Committee.

23.11.'42

Throughout the war, the public were encouraged to purchase
government bonds to help finance the war effort.

11

PUBLIC UTILITY SERVICES

Water and power are vital—and closely intertwined, with pumping facilities to service communities reliant on electricity. But denying water and power to invaders would also deny them to Australian civilians and troops, hurting the defenders as much as it hurt the enemy. As a result, scorched earth planning for utilities was more complicated than it was for resources like factories and mines. So long as civilians remained in an area—which in large population centres meant indefinitely—water and electricity had to remain available. In rural towns slated for evacuation, scorched earth plans were to be carried out only as the last civilians left. These plans focused less on destroying water supplies and power plants than on rendering their output unavailable by cutting or smashing pumps and main pipes, and wrecking turbines, substations and power lines. Decisions about which equipment to target and how best to destroy it were left largely to local authorities who owned or ran the utilities and were thoroughly familiar with their workings.

SCORCHED EARTH

Army Given Full Power

CANBERRA, Monday. -- The Army was given power to carry out a scorched earth policy in Australia by amendments to National Security Regulations gazetted to-day.

An official statement issued with the amendments explains that recent events in the war in the Far East make it essential that the regulations be amended to ensure more effective control of the civil population in an area where evacuation is decided upon, and to make it certain that the Army has the necessary power to carry out a scorched earth policy when necessary.

The principal new provisions are:

(1) Power to prohibit a person from departing from the area to be evacuated without permission.

(2) Prohibition of the return of evacuees to an evacuated area, except with the approval of the authority concerned.

(3) Power to remove or destroy animals, buildings, structures, installations, works, aerodromes, roads, railways, mines, reservoirs or substances which are likely to be useful to an enemy in the event of an area being occupied by him.

HOW CIVILIANS CAN HELP

By Our Defence Correspondent.

Plans to ensure that nothing of use to the enemy is left for him if he invades Australia are rapidly being completed.

Authorities emphasise, however, that these plans will not exempt the individual citizen from responsibility for doing his bit to prevent the Japanese from capturing anything that can be used against us, and from staying put until told to move.

DENIAL OF RESOURCES TO THE ENEMY.
DENIAL CODE, N.S.W. L. OF C. AREA.

PUBLIC UTILITY SERVICES.

      (i) Water
      (ii) Electricity.
      (iii) Gas.

This grouping is made because of the inter-connection of water supply systems with power sources, and because certain power sources are themselves dependent on water supplies.

Military reasons: The denial of gas comes under the basic principle that nothing should be left to the enemy that will help his military efforts. The by-products of gas-making, as well as gas-coal stocks, would be particularly valuable to him.

The denial of water and electricity, however, is in a class by itself. Water can only be denied in instances where the military authorities order an area to be evacuated by civilians and troops; the denial of electricity must not interfere with water supplies in areas where the civilians are required to "stay put".

Installations:

In the Appendix to this Plan are listed:-
A. Gravitation Water Supplies.
B. Water Supplies (Pumping Schemes).
C. The Areas supplied with Water by the Metropolitan Water, Sewerage & Drainage Board; and
D. Electric Power Stations,

within 100 miles of the Coast of N.S.W., and to
which this Operational Plan applies.

The controlling authorities (Water Boards, Shire,
Municipal and County Councils) are shown in the case
of each system or station, and these Agencies are
required to formulate Scorched Earth Plans, and make
arrangements so that if required these Plans can be
implemented at last moment military signal or command.

In the case of gas, the Gas Companies or
Municipalities themselves will be the responsible
agencies.

Operational Plan Principles:

(i)   Water: So long as the principle is accepted
        and enforced that the citizen who finds
        himself in town and city areas must "stay-
        put" - this being a necessary military
        precaution - he cannot be denied a supply
        of water. Failure of water supplies was one
        of the reasons for the capitulation of both
        Hongkong and Singapore, and the Government
        could not contemplate a similar voluntary
        denial in Australia, a denial that would
        react as harshly on the citizen as on the
        enemy, and one which would be of little
        practical value if the denial or productive
        capacity in industry had been fully
        implemented.
        The denial of water will therefore be
        confined to areas that have to be evacuated.
        (a) Cities and towns - Should the military
            necessity arise for the complete
            evacuation of any urban areas, water may
            then be denied to the enemy. This would be
            done only under orders from the Army and
            the work will come under the supervision

of the Public Works Department in Country
areas, or the Metropolitan Water Sewerage
and Drainage Board for the Sydney
Metropolitan Area, or the Hunter District
Water Board for Newcastle.

(b) Rural communities - Small communities
might decide to migrate before an
advancing enemy - most likely into the
bush. Such evacuations could not be
prevented, and it is therefore important
that members of such communities, whether
villages or stations, should understand
their duty and take steps to deny easily-
won supplies of water if they withdraw
of their own volition. This will be the
responsibility of the individual. (See
also Citizen Code).

(ii)   Electricity: The actual denial of electrical
power is less important than the denial of
the plan it drives; and any denial that is
necessary to supplement other plans must be
carried out with circumspection.

Denial of electricity should therefore
work back from the factory workshop.
Electric plant in these places is dealt
with under the Industrial and Manufacturing
Plan and the most effective denial possible
is demanded. Power lines and sectional
transformer stations no longer required will
then be dealt with, and the process will
continue until the power station itself is
in danger of falling into enemy hands when
its destruction will be undertaken. (If,
however, the power station earlier comes
into danger, it must be put out of action).
Plans should whenever possible aim at the

maintenance of electric pumps on water
distribution systems to the last.

(iii)   Gas: This is principally used as a source
of heat for domestic purposes and to that
extent is unimportant militarily, but the by-
products of its manufacture along with the
stocks of gas-coal are of great use in war.
The degree of denial must be decided on for
each locality.

DENIAL METHODS:

(i)   Water:

(a)   Gravitational mains: In towns supplied
by gravitational main from a pipe-
head weir or dam, denial can be most
effectively brought about by smashing as
much of the main as possible and running
the water to waste:

(i)   Fibrolite and cast-iron mains -
smash (after draining if
necessary).

(ii)   Wood-stave mains - cut metal
bindings.

(iii) Steel (welded or rivetted) -
cut exposed sections with oxy-
acetylene or remove supports where
line crosses gullies.

(b)   Pumping schemes: Where delivery depends
on pumps, the most effective denial will
be obtained by destroying motors and
pumps.

(i)   Electric motors - smash end casing
with sledge hammer and make up a
fire of oily waste or the like to
burn out insulation of windings or
otherwise destroy windings.

(ii)   Pumps - remove and conceal
essential parts or smash pumps
with sledge hammers.

(ii)   Electricity:
The means of applying power to productive
machinery require first attention.
Destroy power lines and sectional
transformers.
When it becomes necessary to demolish
the power station explosives may not be
available. In such case the plans shall be
made for the complete denial by simple means.
Suggested simple methods follow:-
Steam turbines - allow water to be carried
over with steam to destroy blades;
or
Shut off lubricating oil supply, put safety
devices out of action and run over-speeded;
or
Remove and hide, or smash essential parts.
Boilers - drain water and maintain fire under
dry boiler;
or
Screw down safety valve, smash feed pump and
leave with large fire;
or
Place gelignite charge in tubes or fire box.
Oil engines - destroy governor, smash
cylinder heads or remove and conceal
essential parts;
or
Make a fire around machinery using oil stocks
as main fuel.
Generators - make up fires around generators
with the object of destroying windings, or
remove and conceal essential parts.

Switchboards - smash.

Hydro-electric plants. Denial of such plants should not be based on cutting off the water power. Turbines, and generators and other purely electrical apparatus should be demolished as the means of denial.

(iii) Gas: The following are suggested denial methods:-

Boosters - wreck by jamming governor and opening throttle valve.

Exhausters - smash in end covers (this is most effective while running).

Washer-scrubbers - fire explosive near base and adjacent to gas inlet.

Gas-holders - puncture and ignite escaping gas.

Coal Stocks - destroy by fire, assisted by inflammable liquids.

Note: Each authority should have ready for invasion emergency, its own plan of denial for its installation, so that if military necessities require, they may readily implement the denial at last moment command.

The above are notes for the guidance of authorities in the preparation of their own plans and organisation.

E.H.F. SWAIN,
Chairman.
Scorched Earth Sub-Committee.
State (N.S.W.) War Effort Co-ordination Committee.

APPENDIX A.
GRAVITATION WATER SUPPLIES.

Town.	Source of Supply.	Controlling Authority.
Armidale.	Dumaresq Creek and Puddledock Creek.	Armidale City Council.
Ballina.	Duck Creek.	Ballina Municipal Council.
Bathurst.	Winburndale Creek (also pumping supply).	Bathurst City Council.
Berry.	Learys Creek (pipehead) (also pumping supply).	Berry Municipal Council.
Bolong	Jaspers Creek (pipehead).	" " "
Grafton & Sth. Grafton.	Nymboida River.	Grafton and South Grafton Water Board.
Jamberoo.	Hyams Creek.	Jamberoo Municipal Council.
Kiama.	Fountaindale Creek.	Kiama Municipal Council.
Lithgow.	Farmers Creek and Middle River (also pump supply under construction).	Lithgow Municipal Council.
Mt Victoria.	Blackheath Service Reservoir (filled by pumping).	Blue Mountains Shire Council.
Mullumbimbi.	Wilsons Creek.	Mullumbimbi Municipal Council.
Murrurundi.	Page River.	Murrurundi Municipal Council.

Murwillumbah.	Kurrumbin Creek (also pumping supply)	Murwillumbah Municipal Council.
Narooma.	Dromedary Creek.	Eurobodalla Shire Council.
Nowra.	Good Dog Creek (also pumping supply).	Nowra Municipal Council.
Portland.	Back Creek (also subartesian supply).	Blaxland Shire Council.
Picton.	Bargo River.	Wollondilly Shire Council.
Tweed Heads.	Coolangatta – Nerang authority.	Tweed Shire Council.
Wauchope.	Blue Creek.	Hastings Shire Council.
Newcastle.	Chichester River.	Hunter District Water Board.

APPENDIX B.
WATER SUPPLIES (PUMPING SCHEMES).

Town.	Source of Supply.	Controlling Authority.
Aberdeen.	Drift Well near Hunter River.	Upper Hunter Shire Ccl.
Bathurst.	Macquarie River (also Grav. supply).	Bathurst City Council.
Bega.	Well in Bega River.	Bega Municipal Council.
Bellingen.	Drift well near Bellinger River.	Bellingen Shire Council.
Berry.	Broughton Creek (also Grav. supply).	Berry Municipal Council.
Blackheath.	Storage on Adams Creek.	Blackheath Mun. Council
Bomaderry.	Bomaderry Creek.	Berry Municipal Council.
Bombala.	Storage on Coolumbooka River.	Bombala Municipal Ccl.
Bowral.	Storage on Wingecarribee Swamp.	Bowral Municipal Council.
Burradoo.	Bulk purchase from Bowral.	Nattai Shire Council.
Casino.	Richmond River.	Casino Municipal Council.
Coff's Harbour.	Orara River.	Dorrigo Shire Council, Coramba.
Cooma.	Murrumbidgee River.	Cooma Municipal Council.

Town.	Source of Supply.	Controlling Authority.
Crookwell.	Dam on Back Creek.	Crookwell Shire Council.
Dungog.	Williams River.	Dungog Municipal Council.
Glen Innes.	Storage on Beardy River.	Glen Innes Munic. Council.
Gloucester.	Gloucester River & Barrington River.	Gloucester Shire Council.
Gosford.	Mooney Mooney Creek.	Gosford Municipal Council.
Goulburn.	Storage on Sooley Creek and Weirs on Wollondilly River.	Goulburn City Council.
Katoomba.	Storages on Cascade Creek.	Katoomba Municipal Ccl.
Kempsey.	Drift Well on Macleay River.	Kempsey Municipal Council.
Kyogle.	Richmond River.	Kyogle Shire Council.
Lismore.	Wilsons Creek.	Lismore Municipal Council.
Lithgow.	Bungleboori Creek (under construction) (also Grav. Supply).	Lithgow Municipal Council.
Medlow Bath.	Adams Creek Storage.	Blackheath Munic. Council.
Mittagong.	Nattai Creek.	Nattai Shire Council.

Town.	Source of Supply.	Controlling Authority.
Moss Vale.	Bong Bong Creek Storage.	Wingecarribee Shire Ccl.
Murwillumbah.	Tweed River (also Grav. supply).	Murwillumbah Municipal Council.
Muswellbrook.	Hunter River.	Muswellbrook Munic. Ccl.
Nowra.	Flat Rock Creek (also Grav. supply).	Nowra Municipal Council.
Penrith.	Nepean River.	Penrith Municipal Council.
Portland.	Subartesian (also Grav. supply).	Blaxland Shire Council.
Queanbeyan.	Cotter River.	Bulk from A.C.T.
Quirindi.	Drift Well on Quirindi Ck.	Quirindi Municipal Council.
Scone.	Drift Well on Kingdon Ponds Creek.	Scone Municipal Council.
Singleton.	Infiltration Wells on Hunter River.	Singleton Municipal Council.
Taree.	Dingo Creek.	Taree-Wingham Water Board Taree.
Tenterfield.	Tenterfield Creek.	Tenterfield Municipal Ccl.
Uralla.	Kentucky Creek.	Gostwyck Shire, Uralla.
Windsor.	Hawkesbury River.	Windsor Municipal Ccl.

Town.	Source of Supply.	Controlling Authority.
Wingham.	See Taree.	
Wyong.	Wyong Creek.	Erina Shire Gosford.
Yass.	Yass River.	Yass Municipal Council.
Bullaburra. Leura. Hazelbrook. Lawson. Wentworth Falls Woodford.	Central Blue Mountains Villages. Emergency Supply from Wentworth Creek.	Blue Mountains Shire Council Lawson.
Faulconbridge. Lindon. Springwood.	Lower Blue Mountains Villages. Pumping from Woodford Creek Storage.	Blue Mountains Shire Council.
Hunter District.	Walcha Scheme.	Hunter River Water Board.

MINOR SYSTEMS.

Name.	Source of Supply.	Authority.
Milson & Rabbit Island.	Small Storage Dam.	Health Department.
Morisset Mental Hospital.	Duck Creek Storages.	" "
Scheyville Training Farm, Windsor.	Hawkesbury River.	Department of Labour & Industry
Waterfall Sanatorium.	Waratah Riverlet Storage.	Health Department.

APPENDIX C.
Areas Supplied by Metropolitan Water, Sewerage and Drainage Board
Metropolitan Water Supply – City of Sydney and Suburbs.

Wollongong & South Coast Water Supply – Austinmer, Balgownie, Bulli, Clifton, Coledale, Corrimal, Dapto, Fairy Meadow, Fern Hill, Fig Tree, Keiraville, Kembla Heights, Mangerton, Mount Keira, Mount Kembla, Port Kembla, Reidtown, Russell Vale, Scarborough, Tarrawanna, Thirroul, Unanderra, Wollongong, Woonona.

Woronora Scheme – Burraneer, Caringbah, Cronulla, Engadine, Miranda, Sutherland.

Country Water Supplies – Campbelltown, Liverpool, Smithfield and Fairfield, Camden, Ingleburn, Minto, Blacktown, St. Marys, Riverstone, Asquith, Mt. Colah, Brooklyn, Menangle and North Menangle, West Fairfield, Raby, Austral-Hoxton Park, Hills District, Richmond.

APPENDIX D.
ELECTRIC POWER STATIONS.

Name.	Authority.	Capacity K.Ws.	Type.
Sydney.	Department of Railways.	201,000	Steam.
Newcastle.	do.	45,500	do.
Lithgow.	do.	10,000	do.
Burrinjuck.	Department of Public Works.	20,000	Hydro.
Port Kembla.	do.	14,500	Steam.
Sydney.	County Council.	225,000	do.
Clarence River.	do.	8,300	Oil & Hydro.
Bega Valley.	do.	482	Oil.
Armidale.	Municipal Council.	1,120	Gas & Oil.
Cooma.	do.	332	Oil.
Glen Innes.	do.	840	Oil.
Katoomba.	do.	1,725	Steam.
Mullumbimby.	do.	645	Oil & Hydro.
Murwillumbah.	do.	925	Steam
Newcastle.	Newcastle (City) Council.	3,500	Steam.
Port Macquarie.	do.	324	Oil.
Quirindi.	do.	330	Steam & Oil.
Tamworth.	do.	4,300	Steam.
Tenterfield.	do.	364	Oil.
Crookwell.	Shire Council.	202	Gas & Oil.

Name.	Authority.	Capacity K.Ws.	Type.
Dorrigo.	do.	344	Oil & Hydro
Ballina.	Electric Construction Co. of Aust.	970	Oil.
Bellbird.	Hetton Bellbird Collieries Ltd.	2,000	Steam.
Berrima.	Southern Portland Cement Ltd.	3,750	Steam.
Bombala.	Bombala Elect. Supply.	200	Oil.
Braidwood.	Braidwood Elect. Supply Co.	48	Oil.
Cessnock.	Caledonian Collieries Ltd.	13,222	Steam.
Eden	Eden Electricity Supply.	57	Oil.
Guyra.	Guyra Electric Supply Co.	116	Oil.
Illawarra Nth.	Corrimal Coal & Coke Pty. Ltd.	1,960	Steam.
Kempsey.	Kempsey Electric Light & Power Co. Ltd.	568	Oil.
Merriwa.	M. Campbell & Co.	94	Oil.
Milton.	E.H. Riley.		Oil.

Name.	Authority.	Capacity K.Ws.	Type.
Moruya.	Moruya Electrical Supply Co.	55	Oil.
Murrurundi.	The Murrurundi Electric Supply Co. Ltd.	89	Oil.
Narooma.	Narooma Electricity Supply Co. Pty. Ltd.	112	Oil.
Oberon.	A.F. Anstiss.	63	Oil.
Pambula.	Godfrey's Motors Ltd.	12	Oil.
Tuncurry.	Cape Hawke District Rural Co-op. Society Ltd.		Oil.
Wauchope.	Wauchope Electric Supply Ltd.	92	Oil.
Sydney.	Electric Light & Power Supply Corp. Ltd.	41,750	Steam.
Weston.	Hebburn Collieries Ltd.	3,000	Steam.

14.11.'42

12

ORGANISATION OF SCORCHED EARTH SUPPORT SQUADS

Scorched Earth Support Squads were formed to help instruct and train members of the public in the content of the Scorched Earth policy and the specific measures needed to implement it. Sound knowledge of the terrain and local resources that might prove useful to the enemy was important, so these squads were composed mostly of local residents. In most cases, they were formed around local fire brigades and Volunteer Defence Corps units at centres such as Lismore, Grafton, Coffs Harbour, Taree, Bega, Tamworth, Singleton and Tenterfield.

When this Happens

... will you know what to do?

It will be too late to ask questions when the bombs begin to fall. Find out **NOW** what you must do in an air raid — what you can do to help your local Warden. See, too, that your family is thoroughly familiar with elementary first aid, the location of the nearest shelter, how to extinguish incendiary bombs. Their lives — and yours — may depend on it . . .

ORGANISATION OF SCORCHED EARTH
SUPPORT SQUADS.

NOTES FOR THE GUIDANCE OF ORGANISING OFFICERS:

Generally - and subject to any revision that may be found desirable as a result of development experience - the arrangements for Scorched Earth Support Squad organisation will be as follows:-

1. North and South Coast to be visited and organised westward to the edge of the tableland, (Port Stephens - Port Kembla defended areas excepted), but including the Singleton-New England Highway centres to Wallangarra.

2. Possible extension of organisation subsequently.

3. Coast Scorched Earth Support Squad Areas will usually correspond with V.D.C. battalion areas, as follows:-

   (i)   Queensland border south to Evans Head and Ampledale on the railway (1 V.D.C. battalion).

   (ii)   Thence south to Corindi and Glenreagh (2 V.D.C. battalion).

   (iii) Thence south to Telegraph Point (16 V.D.C. battalion).

   (iv)   Thence south to Port Stephens and Martin's Creek on the railway (4 V.D.C. battalion).

   (v)   Wollongong to Victorian Border (13, 14 and 15 V.D.C. battalion.

   (vi)   Singleton-Tenterfield (Eastern parts of 6 V.D.C. and 3 V.D.C. battalion areas) Scorched Earth operations will be restricted at present to the coastal area up to the edge of the tableland and to the Singleton-Tenterfield area.

4. V.D.C. commanders should be contacted:-

Lismore   Capt. T. Dwyer, M.C., 31 Second Av.,
             Lismore.

Grafton   Lt. Col. E.A. Woodward, Grafton.

Coffs Hbr.   T.C. Johnston, Karangi, via Coffs
             Harbour (sector headquarters at
             Kempsey).

Taree   Lt. S.K. Lipscombe, Taree (sector
             headquarters at Wauchope).

Bega   T.W. Walcott, Bombala (sector
             headquarters Bega, Cooma, Wagga).

Tamworth   Lt. Col. H.F. White, C.M.G., D.S.O.
             (sector headquarters Narrabri,
             Tamworth, Scone).

5. The police officer in each locality should
   also be contacted. The Commissioner for Police
   has been informed fully of the Scorched Earth
   proposals through Police Inspector Standen,
   who is a member of the Scorched Earth Committee
   and no doubt will issue suitable directions
   to members of the Police Force throughout the
   territory covered.

6. Public Servants might also be contacted. (The
   Chairman of the Sub-Committee, as Commissioner
   for Forests, has asked all forest officers to
   collaborate with the Scorched Earth organisers).

7. Two officers of each S.E.S.S. area, in company,
   but dividing the work: Responsibility will be
   to the Board of Fire Commissioners of N.S.W.,
   representing the State War Effort Co-Ordination
   Committee (Scorched Earth Sub-Committee, the
   Secretary and official address of which is
   "Forestry Commission, Presbyterian Assembly
   Building, York and Margaret Streets, Sydney".)

8. A "Scorched Earth Code" (State War Effort Co-
   Ordination Committee - N.S.W.) has been prepared

for the guidance of Scorched Earth Support Squad
officers: copies are supplied; for distribution
only to responsible persons collaborating in
Scorched Earth operations.

9. S.E.S.S. officers will call upon the Local
Governing Authorities, present their
credentials; will explain the "Scorched Earth
Code" and invite collaboration, particularly
from (i) governmental and local governmental
authorities; (ii) principal trades, industries
&c. (The Premier's Department will write
beforehand to the Mayors and Presidents of
such authorities, briefly advising them of the
projected visits and their purpose).
Help should be sought also in the provision
of any necessary office accommodation, and if
possible local transport.

10. The local Fire Brigades will form the Scorched
Earth Support Squad nucleus, co-opting selected
local volunteers. Where there is no Fire
Brigade, viz. outside the present jurisdiction
of the Board of Fire Commissioners of N.S.W., the
organisers will form a subsidiary Scorched Earth
Support Squad having liaison with the nearest
Fire Brigade.

11. The duties of the S.E.S.S. Squads will be:
  (i)   To explain the principles of the Scorched
        Earth Code.
  (ii) To secure understanding and responsible
        local collaboration towards implementing
        prior preparations in case of invasion
        emergency.
  (iii) To lay emphasis that the work at present
        being undertaken is one of preparation,
        and that the actual denial operation will
        only operate in the last extremity, and

then only by decision of the Military.
Further, that it is most necessary that
preparation should take place everywhere,
as it cannot be known where the enemy will
strike.

(iv)   To encourage steady and determined civil
       morale.

(v)   To contact Governmental representatives,
       and representatives of local industry,
       trade and business, and keep the State
       War Effort Co-Ordination Committee Sub-
       Committee fully informed, by separate
       reports on problems as they arise, and by
       weekly progress reports of the work of
       preparation and the degree of readiness
       for action at local military command.

(vi)   To contact the local military command,
       to ensure that military orders will
       be properly and instantly conveyed to
       all concerned, without danger of fifth
       columnism, precipitate action or sabotage
       &c.

(vii) To see that in extremity the operations
       commanded by the military are completely
       and successfully carried out, even if they
       are compelled to personally take action.

(viii) Generally to ensure collaboration with
       the operation of the Scorched Earth Code.

   Necessary transport facilities will be
provided by S.W.E.C.C., Premier's Office.

Note: The assistance of each administration,
       service, business, trade and industry &c.
       is sought to carry out its own Scorched
       Earth planning and operation, but units
       should endeavor to secure uniform and
       co-ordinated methods &c.

The S.E.S.S. first job is to teach and police and organise; and if invasion comes, to act as supports to citizens to ensure effective completion of military orders.

The whole organisation is one of civil collaboration with Army in the defence of our shores.

Should any of those instructions, or the Code itself, prove, after experience, to need revision or elaboration, the organising S.E.S.S. officers will report accordingly.

Organising officers will not commit the State to any expenditure.

SPECIAL: THE EXTREME URGENCY OF THE MATTER MUST BE EMPHASISED. INSTANT ACTION IS ESSENTIAL - AND ANY TENDENCIES TO PANIC MUST BE DEALT WITH.

EXTRA SPECIAL: SABOTAGE: THE QUESTION OF SABOTAGE AND FIFTH COLUMN ACTIVITIES MUST BE CAREFULLY CONSIDERED.

NOTES

TIMELINE

1   This timeline draws substantially on *The Home Front, Family Album: Remembering Australia 1939–45,* introduced by Nancy Keesing, Weldon, Sydney, 1991.

INTRODUCTION

1   The reality of this threat has been questioned by several historians, including Peter Stanley in, for example, '"He's Not Coming South": The invasion that wasn't', presented at the Canberra conference 'Remembering 1942' in 2002. However, watching Japanese forces overrun one country after another to their north, Australians 'had every right to entertain this fear, and little reason to believe otherwise,' as Stanley himself notes in 'Dramatic Myth and Dull Truth: Invasion by Japan in 1942', in Craig Stockings (ed.), *Zombie Myths of Australian History.* The Scorched Earth Policy presented here was intended to address that possibility.

2   W.J. McKell, NSW Premier, to W.F. Dunn, Minister for Agriculture and Forests, 16 February 1942, in State Records NSW: Forestry Registered Files, Series 4271, File No. 24090, Pt 3 at 3/5944.

3   Secret Circular from Prime Minister J. Curtin to W.J. McKell, NSW Premier, 30 July 1942, in State Records NSW: Forestry Registered Files, Series 4271, File No. 24090, Pt 3 at 3/5944.

4   *Ibid.* See also National Archives of Australia: Evacuation: Scorched Earth Policy, Series A453, Control Symbol 1942/51/848.

5   Denial of Resources to the Enemy, Directive for Guidance in the Formulation of Detailed Plans, in National Archives of Australia, *ibid*.

6   Australia's total population in 1941 was approximately 7 million people; NSW had 2.8 million, Victoria 1.9 million and Queensland 1 million.

7   W.J. McKell, NSW Premier, to W.F. Dunn, Minister for Agriculture and Forests, 16 February 1942.

8   E.H.F. Swain, NSW Forestry Commissioner, to W.J. McKell, NSW Premier, 16 February 1942, in State Records NSW: Forestry Registered Files, Series 4271, File No. 24090, Pt 3 at 3/5944; W.J. McKell, NSW

Premier, to H.P. Lazzarini, Minister for Home Security, 13 April 1942, at AA: Series 453, Item 1942/51/848.

9   See Peter Grose's discussion of the numbers in *An Awkward Truth: The bombing of Darwin, February 1942*, Allen & Unwin, Sydney, 2009, Ch. 15.

10 See Michael McKernan, *All In! Fighting the War at Home*, Allen & Unwin, Sydney, 1983, for more comprehensive analysis.

11 W.J. McKell to H.P. Lazzarini, Minister for Home Security, 13 April 1942.

CHAPTER 1

1   L.T. Carron, 'Swain, Edward Harold (1883–1970)', *Australian Dictionary of Biography*, National Centre of Biography, Australian National University, http://adb.anu.edu.au/biography/swain-edward-harold-8723/text15273, published first in hardcopy 1990, accessed online 19 June 2016.

2   Peter Holzworth, *A Tribute to Edward Harold Fulcher Swain*, 2015 (self-published), pp. 104–5.

3   Thomas (Tom) Wintringham (1898–1949), a veteran of the Spanish Civil War, published numerous books and articles calling on Britons to prepare for a guerrilla 'people's war' in the event of a German invasion.

4   John Dedman, also a member of the War Cabinet.

5   A cumbersome producer unit could be fitted to the back of motor vehicles to burn solid fuel, such as wood or coal, to manufacture gas as a substitute for petrol.

6   APC powder is aspirin-phenacetin-caffeine (Bex).

7   Melasol is tea tree oil.

8   Australia Day.

9   In the Spanish Civil War.

10 Tom Wintringham, *New Ways of War*, Penguin, 1940.

11 Russian emigre John Alexander Youhotsky was a water engineer who died in 1946.

12 Japanese forces seized oilfields in Borneo and airfields in Celebes (now Sulawesi), on either side of the Macassar Strait, in January 1942.

CHAPTER 2

1   When German forces reached the Dnieper River industrial area in
    August 1941, the Soviets destroyed the huge dam at Zhaporozhye,
    80 kilometres south of Dnipropetrovsk.
2   Manchukuo was a Japanese puppet state in north-east China
    (Manchuria) and inner Mongolia. (1932–1945).
3   Subversion by cells of enemy agents or sympathisers.

CHAPTER 4

1   In early 1942, Australia's state- and territory-based military districts
    were renamed Line of Communication Areas.
2   United Nations here means the Allies; the UN as we know it did not
    exist at this time.
3   A.N. 60 was a common brand of gelignite used in mining and
    construction.

CHAPTER 5

1   Colonial Sugar Refining Company.
2   North Coast Steam Navigation Company.
3   Foley Bros was a butter factory.
4   R.J. White and Co. were timber merchants.
5   Brown Ltd were timber and Pacific shipping agents.
6   Maxwell Porter was a sawmill; Wright Bros almost certainly was
    as well.
7   In Bateman's Bay, both Mitchell Bros and Fennings were sawmills.
8   In the original, this appeared as 'Bucken Bour Junct'.
9   In the original, this appeared as Noorooma; the town name officially
    changed to Narooma in the 1970s.

CHAPTER 6

1   'Immobilisation of Small Craft', Hansard, House of Representatives
    (Canberra), 29 April 1942, at http://historichansard.net/hofreps/
    1942/19420429_reps_16_170/.
2   *Ibid.*

ACKNOWLEDGEMENTS

The Scorched Earth policy reproduced here has survived thanks to the diligence of the archivists employed at State Records NSW. In my experience there are a number of outstanding individuals who have a deep knowledge of the records and the historic peculiarities that mark the various systems of management pervading government record keeping since 1788. Their commitment is evidenced by their long years of service in a job they obviously love. I wish to especially acknowledge Gail Davis, Wendy Gallagher, Emily Hanna and Janette Pelosi.

In getting this book into print much is owed to the encouragement of my friends and colleagues, Janet Gough and David Andor. Without their pushing and shoving the policy may not have reached the broad audience now possible. The team at Allen & Unwin—led by publisher Elizabeth Weiss and editorial manager Angela Handley have very ably, sympathetically and efficiently worked to a very tight deadline. It's a miracle.

Lastly, I wish to thank my husband David Rosen who undertook the scanning of the original files, picture research and copyright clearances; he's been a slave to history for almost 40 years, and deserves the sympathy of all.

PHOTO CREDITS

p. i: *The Australian Women's Weekly,* 14 March 1942, cover. <http://nla.gov.au/nla.news-page4721213>.

p. vi: Edward Harold Fulcher Swain, courtesy of Peter Holzworth.

p. x: *Daily Mirror,* 8 December 1941.

p. xv (and repeated): Japanese air force poster (detail of planes), Getty Images.

p. xx: 'Citizen "Guerillas" training for bush warfare', *The Sydney Morning Herald,* 2 February 1942, <http://nla.gov.au/nla.news-article17786030>.

p. 3 (and repeated): background, Shutterstock.

p. 41: *The Australian Women's Weekly,* 20 December 1941, <http://nla.gov.au/nla.news-page4716326>.

p. 49: *The Australian Women's Weekly,* 17 January 1942, <http://nla.gov.au/nla.news-page4720570>.

p. 66: Norman Lindsay, *The Bulletin,* 1942.

p. 76: *The Australian Women's Weekly,* 14 March 1942, <http://nla.gov.au/nla.news-page4721221>.

p. 86: *The Australian Women's Weekly,* 7 February 1942, <http://nla.gov.au/nla.news-page4720671>.

p. 95: 'Unity Means Victory', *The Sydney Morning Herald,* 21 March 1942, <http://nla.gov.au/nla.news-page1107554>.

p. 108: 'The Shelling of Sydney', *Argus,* 1942, State Library of Victoria.

p. 120: Australian War Memorial, image no. RC00811.

p. 128: *The Australian Women's Weekly,* 27 December 1941, <http://nla.gov.au/nla.news-page4718995>.

p. 138: National Archives of Australia, C934, 10.

p. 147: *The Sydney Morning Herald,* 11 December 1941, <http://nla.gov.au/nla.news-page1106374>.

p. 157: National Archives of Australia, Image no. C934, 154.

p. 168: *The Australian Women's Weekly,* 24 January 1942, <http://nla.gov.au/nla.news-page4721885>.

p. 179: *The Australian Women's Weekly,* 21 March 1942, <http://nla.gov.au/nla.news-page4719837>.

p. 198: Australian War Memorial, image no. P04262.003.

p. 208: Lindsay family photo, courtesy Angela Handley.

p. 218: Australian War Memorial, image no. ART90964, courtesy Katrina Perryman.

p. 223: Australian War Memorial, image no. 128108.

p. 232: *The Bulletin,* 1942.

p. 238: Australian War Memorial, image no. 027267.

p. 240: Australian War Memorial, image no. 042825.

p. 248: Australian War Memorial, image no. ARTV06690.

p. 254: *The Sydney Morning Herald,* 20 February 1942, <http://nla.gov.au/nla.news-page1107224>.

p. 256: *The Sydney Morning Herald,* 10 March 1942, <http://nla.gov.au/nla.news-page1107428>.

p. 274: *The Sydney Morning Herald,* 2 April 1942, <http://nla.gov.au/nla.news-page1093345>.

Photo section:

p. 1: Australian War Memorial, image no. ARTV09225-1.

pp. 2–3: *The Australian Women's Weekly,* 21 February 1942, <http://nla.gov.au/nla.news-page4719939>.

p. 4: State Library of Victoria.

p. 5: *The Australian Women's Weekly,* 7 February 1942, <http://nla.gov.au/nla.news-page4720654>.

p. 6: National Archives of Australia, MP891/31, 3.

p. 7: Australian Army, *Wollongong, New South Wales* (rev. 2nd edn), printed by A.H.Q. Cartographic Company, Melbourne, 1942. National Library of Australia, http://trove.nla.gov.au/version/175596608.

p. 8: National Archives of Australia, MP1472/1 part 2.